Hiking the
Real Estate Trail
Field Guide

Also by Terry Wilson

BOOK:
Hiking the Real Estate Trail:
From Classroom to Trailhead
A planning and preparation book for new and
experienced agents.

CD AUDIO SET:
Hiking the Real Estate Trail:
Your study guide for the
N.C. Real Estate Exam
This CD set is the perfect complimentary
study guide for the pre-license and
N.C. Real Estate licensing exams.

Terry Wilson is passionate about educating
and mentoring real estate agents. He teaches
pre- and post-licensing and CE Real Estate classes
and is broker/owner of Wilson Realty, Co.

Contents

Your journey
begins

Introduction

*Nothing, and
I mean
NOTHING
is more
important than
generating leads.*

I wrote a book for new and experienced agents called *Hiking the Real Estate Trail*. It's chock full of information to help you get your business up and running or keep it going. What it lacked, however, was a field guide that you could take on the hike with you. That's the purpose of this guide.

When it comes to real estate, lead generation is a contact sport. This has been and always will be a relationship business. People do business with people they trust and like. Period. Think back to all the times you bought an expensive item. Did you always go with the cheapest provider? Did you buy from the person/company that treated you poorly? We buy from and work with people that we trust, and we like. That's it. Period. End of story.

The trails we take to build those relationships have changed. Now we have social media and texting and blogging, and podcasts and the list goes on… But in the end, it is about generating leads. When it comes to building your real estate career, nothing should ever come before lead generation. Knowing everything about your contracts and your MLS and all the other supporting tools won't help if you don't have anybody to use them on. When you rise from bed each morning, your first thought should be "Who will I talk to today about real estate?"

With that in mind, I have developed this guidebook for you to take along while you hike your real estate trail.

There are hundreds of books and videos and podcasts out there and I'm sure if you carefully follow their guidance you could be quite successful in the world of real estate and I do encourage you to review them for ideas.

However, I'm not going to tell you what to do or how to do it (although I do have some tips for you throughout the guide). Sure, I could tell you that the key to success – and I would argue that it is – is to make 20 phone calls a day and by the end of the week you will have contacted 100 people and by the end of the year 5,200 people, the problem is if you don't see yourself being willing to pick up the phone then these instructions won't help.

There are many ways to build your business; from phone calls to social media, cocktail parties to open houses; seminars, podcasts, TV, radio, door knocking... the list is endless. The key is to find the one or two or even three things that YOU will do. That YOU feel comfortable doing. If you enjoy doing it, then you'll get good at it and if you get good at it then you'll have success in building your business. It's really that simple. The thing is though, only you know what you're good at (or at least what you're willing to get good at) and what you enjoy doing.

....

*The key to success is at the intersection of
the thing you're good at and the thing you enjoy doing.*

....

I used to cold call, and I was good at it, but I hated it. I developed a strong bicep in my left arm because the phone was so heavy! I didn't want to pick it up. I like to teach and (at least I think) I'm pretty good at it. So, there's my intersection. On page 14 you'll find your intersection. By the way, if you want tips and tricks on picking up that heavy phone please refer to chapter 17 in the *Hiking the Real Estate Trail* book.

Whatever you want to do, this guide will help you stay on track. It is not meant to replace other advice books, but to act as a companion to them. It is your field guide. You can carry it with you and jot down what's working and what's not. It will also help you hold yourself accountable. I've tried to make it easy to use so you're not spending all your time updating spreadsheets and calendars and tracking logs. *See a daily sample page that has been filled in on page 24.*

This field guide is set up to run for 66 days. You may have heard it takes 21 days to develop a habit and this may be true, but science is discovering it takes a minimum of 66 days to make that habit stick and become the core of who you are. Think about when you brush your teeth. Better yet, don't think about it because you don't; it's just a part of you. We must consciously choose to perform a habit, but we don't once it becomes a part of us. If you miss a day here and there don't skip pages, just make a note and keep going.

Find an accountability buddy (not your spouse! Trust me on this one). Hold each other accountable. It works. It's a pain sometimes, but it works!!

Why hike the trail?

Do you really know why you want to help others buy and sell real estate? Before going deeper into this guide, review the Big Why exercise.

Of all the questions raised when starting a real estate career, this one is probably the most important.

The BIG WHY is what motivates everyone. Professional football players are driven to hurl themselves around the field taking incredible health risks for one BIG WHY – The Super bowl ring. Appalachian Trail (AT) thru-hikers get up every day and hike the 2,175-mile trail in sometimes horrid conditions for one BIG WHY – to experience this: The Northern Terminus at Mt. Katahdin…

Also consider that we live on a small rock that spins on its axis at approximately 1,038 miles per hour; I say approximately because it very much depends on where you are standing right now. As it spins, our little top hurls itself around a distant sun at 67,000 miles per hour – a speed that would allow you to leave Raleigh, NC at 11:57AM and arrive in Los Angeles, CA less than three minutes later - just in time for your noon lunch - Assuming you would still want lunch. Everything you do, you say, and you accomplish, everyone you meet, help, hate and love will all exist in one lifetime on this tiny rock spinning around a relatively small sun at a speed that is amazingly difficult to fathom. I can't think of a better reason than this to understand your BIG WHY.

*It's hard to get up every day and fight the good fight
if you don't know what you're fighting for.*

Helping others buy and sell real estate can be incredibly rewarding and financially lucrative. But it also has as many frustrations and setbacks as the AT. You may already know the BIG WHY. But if you aren't sure what your BIG WHY is, take a few minutes and check out the BIG WHY exercise starting on page 9.

Without knowing your BIG WHY, it is easy to lose focus and wonder why you're dealing with the daily slings and arrows. In other words, it's hard to get up every day and fight the good fight if you don't know what you're fighting for.

Once you know your BIG WHY, make it your laptop's screen saver, and write it on sticky notes all over your house. Put it in your car, your purse, or your wallet. In other words, constantly remind yourself what you are trying to accomplish and why.

Consider this, on July 31st, 2011 Jennifer Pharr Davis, 28, completed the fastest hike of the 2,175-mile Appalachian Trail, averaging 46.9 miles per day. She trimmed 26 hours off the previous record. When asked why she did it, this was her quote:

"I consider it to be a love story. I love the trail and far more than that I love my husband. Beyond romance, I believe true love is best demonstrated through endurance and perseverance. That is what got me through the bad weather, intense pain and many hardships this summer – a devotion to the trail and a complete trust and shared intimacy with my husband."

Now that's a BIG WHY!

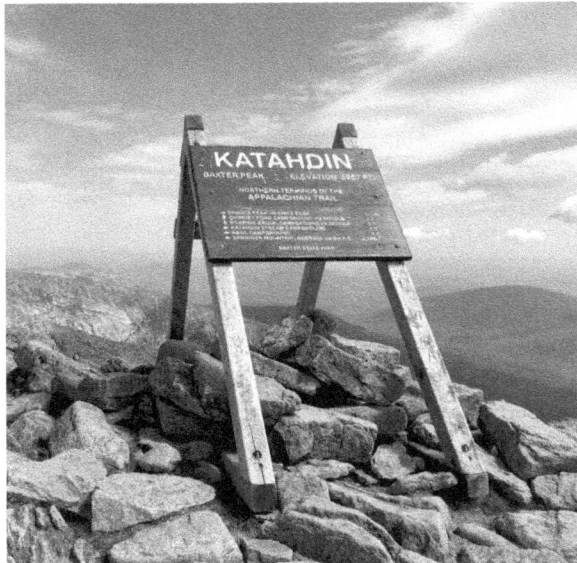

photo: Cathryn McCann

The BIG WHY exercise

German philosopher Frederick Nietzsche once said, "He who has a why can endure any how."

Of all the questions we can ask, the most revealing is "Why?" Like layers of an onion, every time this question is asked another layer of truth is peeled away. Psychologists say we need to ask why five times to get to the truth of something. It would be easy then to list the word "why" five times and ask you to answer that question each time until we uncover your BIG WHY. However, unless I was sitting across from you helping you interpret and build on your answers it would not be terribly effective, so let's try another strategy to uncover your BIG WHY. In working this exercise, go as quickly as you can and don't rule anything out; simply put your thoughts down based on the question asked…

There are thousands of opportunities and career paths, why real estate?

_____

_____

_____

_____

_____

What do I hope to accomplish with my real estate career?

_____

_____

_____

_____

_____

What are the reasons I want to accomplish these things?

_____

_____

_____

_____

Of these reasons, which one is the most important to me?

_____
_____
_____
_____
_____
_____

Why is it more important than the other reasons given?

_____
_____
_____
_____
_____
_____

What would happen if I were not able to accomplish or fulfill this reason?

_____
_____
_____
_____
_____
_____

Is there another field of work that could also fulfill this reason? If so, what is it and why aren't I choosing that career path?

_____
_____
_____
_____
_____
_____

Will I know when I have fulfilled this reason? (Yes or No) What will that look like?

_____

_____

_____

_____

_____

_____

How will I feel and what reward will I give myself when I have fulfilled this reason?

_____

_____

_____

_____

_____

_____

What am I willing to give up to reach my BIG WHY? There are only so many hours in the day.

_____

_____

_____

_____

_____

_____

Finally, what gets me out of bed in the morning?

_____

_____

_____

_____

_____

_____

What did I discover?

Write it here and place it on sticky notes, put a copy in your wallet/purse. Keep an eye on it. You'll want to reference it from time to time.

_____

_____

_____

_____

_____

_____

The answers to these questions will help you paint your BIG WHY picture. Share your findings with those close to you, so they can help you stay on track. Always keep this picture in mind, particularly when times are tough, it is the driving force behind your business.

Now you hopefully know your BIG WHY and regardless of the reason, only you know why you got your real estate license and why you've chosen a career as a real estate agent ready to assist others with buying and selling real property. Whatever your reason, you're at the trail head ready to go.

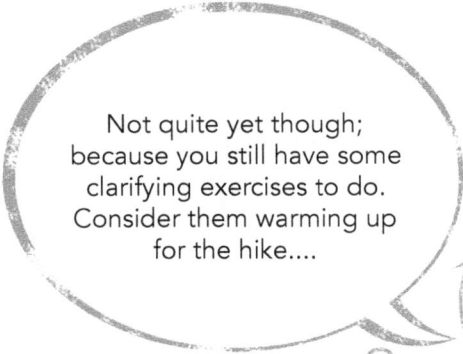

Not quite yet though; because you still have some clarifying exercises to do. Consider them warming up for the hike....

Your intersection

Where's your intersection of
what you like to do and what
you're good at (or are willing
to get good at)?

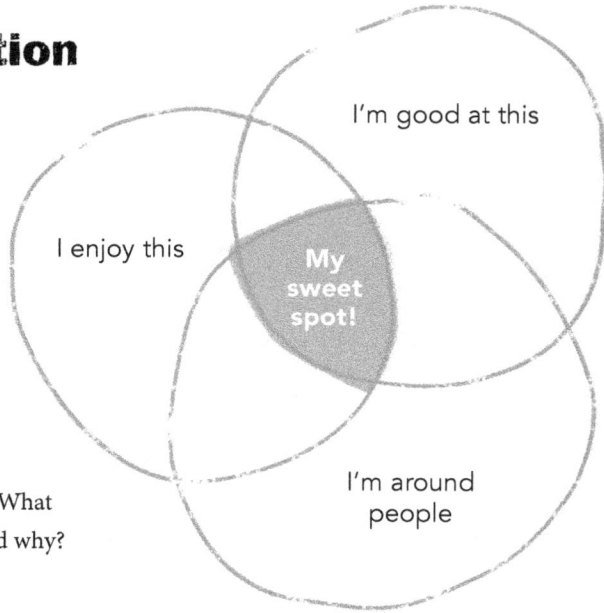

I'm good at this

I enjoy this

My
sweet
spot!

I'm around
people

✓ Think about your past life. What
jobs/activities did you enjoy and why?

✓ What are you good at or want to be good at? I'd teach for free (not forever, but
certainly for an hour or two because I enjoy it). What task would you do for free, if only
for an hour or two?

✓ What do you do for entertainment/hobbies?

✓ Do any of these things get you around other people? If not can you change that?

Your objective is to find your "sweet spot". So, what is your sweet spot? That's where you'll want to stay to achieve your BIG WHY.

....

Ponder the above and think about activities you could do that you would enjoy doing and help you build your contact list.

....

About your guide

I believe there is something very powerful that happens when you put pen/pencil to paper.

The day field is left blank, so you can start anytime. Simply fill in the first day and get hiking. Each morning you will enter the activities for the day and track how you're doing.

If you need ideas for inexpensive or free lead generation ideas, check out page 185. There are 50 ways to build your business (with apologies to Paul Simon)

There is a six-day running total that you'll add to each day, so you can see your progress. Why not seven days? Because everybody needs a day off!!

On the sixth day you'll do a quick review of what went right, what went wrong, what scripts and types of meetings worked, and which didn't. Basically, you're adjusting as you go so you don't get too far down the wrong path before you realize you're lost and frustrated.

I believe there is something very powerful that happens when you put pen/pencil to paper.

Why not just use your calendar on your phone? I believe there is something very powerful that happens when you put pen/pencil to paper. The tactile feel, the time required to handwrite causes you to stop and think. To really get introspective. Typing on a computer or smartphone simply doesn't allow for that. I've tried to design the book to be fun and I encourage you to use different colored pens and/or pencils. You can draw outside of the lines here. I've also designed this guidebook, so you can carry it with you and make quick notes. Each day has a corresponding pondering page, so you can jot down your notes from your phone calls and meetings.

The daily pages of this guide are broken into two sections, the first section (the ☼ symbol) should be done in the morning before you start your day, so you know what trail you're taking and how far you need to hike. The second section (the ☽ symbol) is for you to review in the evening around the campfire to determine how the hike went. I want to stress here that this is a "no shame, no blame" guide. If you didn't accomplish some or any of your goals for the day then learn from it. What will you do different

Your goal is to update this guide every day.

tomorrow? If the answer is nothing, then maybe we've got you working on the wrong things and you'll want to go back and review your intersection. There is no one right way to build your business. Well, there is one right way and that's the way that YOU want to do it.

....

TIP: In the evening lay out what you are going to do tomorrow; that way you don't have to spend any part of tomorrow morning figuring it out. You can just hit the ground running.

....

Remember one thing though, in the end you must have clients and customers to build your business and this takes appointments and to get those appointments you need to reach out to people. Be flexible, do it your way, but if you find that you aren't getting face to face opportunities it's probably time to try something new. On the other side of that same coin though, don't give up too early. If you mail a postcard once and don't get results don't give up. Nobody goes to the gym once and expects to get the body of their dreams; unless, of course, the body you have is the one of your dreams.

Goal setting

Ok, let's face it, money is important. While your BIG WHY may not be about money, it probably takes money to achieve your BIG WHY, so let's talk about money. Only you know your market, so I can't pretend to tell you what the average price of a home sells for, or the average number of homes that fail to sell, or the average days-on-market (DOM), but you'll want to know this information because without it you won't know, on average, how many listings and/or buyers you'll need to reach your financial goal.

1. Desired Annual closed GCI (Gross Commission Income): $ _____

2. Estimated average commission per side: $ _____

3. The number of total closed sales to achieve my income goal: _____
   (number 1 divided by number 2)

4. My annual projected closings will come from: 4.a. Listings sold _____

   4.b. Buyers sold _____

_____% of my listings will sell. Therefore, I need this many listings: _____
(4.a. listings sold divided by % of listings that will sell)

_____% of my listing appointments will result in a listing. Therefore, I need this many listing appointments: _____
(number of listings needed divided by % of listing appointments)

_____% of buyers that will buy. Therefore, I need this many buyer appointments:
(4.b. buyers sold divided by % of buyers who will buy) _____

_____% of my buyer contracts will cancel. Therefore, I need this many buyers:
(buyer appointments divided by (100% minus % of buyers canceled)) _____

....

Don't worry about being exact.
You'll tweak these numbers as you hike.

....

Add the total number of buyer and seller appointments you need and multiply by the number of touches you think it will take to get those buyer and seller appointments.

For example, it may take 10 touches to get one appointment. Therefore, if the number of appointments you need to reach your GCI goal is 100, then 100 x 10 = 1,000. Over the next year you'll need 1,000 touches. Divide 1,000 by 52 and you get approximately 20 touches per week.

....

NOTE: You aren't going to work 52 weeks a year so adjust accordingly. For example, if you plan to take four weeks off to travel to Europe then you'll need to divide your touch number by 48 not 52.

....

With all of that said, don't get too caught up in the numbers. If you are consistently working your lead generation activities daily, these numbers will take care of themselves.

In the table below, you can enter the number of appointments per week and then per month. Remember that you won't work 52 weeks and 12 months a year, so you'll have to take those out and increase the numbers per week or month as needed.

Appointments Goal	Week	Month
Listings		
New buyers		

For a more detailed discussion of goal setting see Chapter 6 in the book *Hiking the Real Estate Trail.*

Now let's talk about the hours available to you throughout the day. Unless you're like my friend Len Elder, there are only 24 hours in a day (apparently his planet has 70 hours per day because I've never seen one man get more done in one day!). Not all 24 hours are available for lead generation and when it comes to real estate, lead generation is your number one priority!

To determine the number of hours you have available for building your business, calculate the number of daily hours you spend on each item below.

Total hours in a day __**24**__

Sleeping _____

With family and friends _____

Eating _____

Fitness and grooming _____

Hours driving _____

Committed to your personal time _____

Hours needed for existing business _____

=

Hours to spend building your business _____

If you're shocked and thinking you can't get it all done in the short amount of time that's available, I'm here to tell you that you can. You just need to be efficient and focused.

After all, if you need to call five people, each phone call shouldn't take more than 5 minutes. So even with dialing that's a maximum of 30 minutes. I'll bet you still have time to do your other lead generating activities. If you don't then consider what you will shift or give up.

Sleep studies are inconclusive as to how much sleep we need. Some say more, some say less. I seem to function better on less sleep. A quick ten-minute cat nap perks me up if I need it. If you need to buy back time, consider the amount of sleep you're getting. A good book on this subject is *The Miracle Morning* by Hal Elrod.

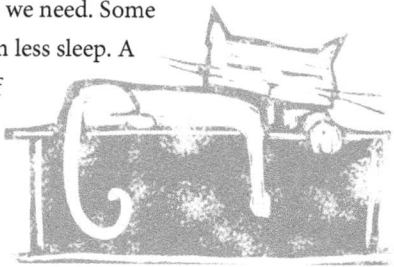

Your personal contract

A contract to myself…

In the interest of my own success I commit to working through this guide each and every day. I may fall down, but I will get back up and hike this trail every day. Even when I know that I'm just not "feeling it" that day, I will push myself to pursue my BIG WHY and do what is necessary to generate leads every single day!

Signed: _____ Date: _____

Let's get started

Sample Day

Date __Tuesday, 6/7/2018__   🏕 10:40 pm   🥤 6:15 am

last night's bedtime   this mornings rise time

Hours available to work lead generation today __1.25__

Activity	Actual	Goal	%	🙂	😐	🙁
phone calls	20	30	67 %	✓		
meet for coffee	1	2	50 %		✓	
lunch w/Marty	1	1	100 %	✓		
note cards	2	10	20 %			✓
Totals	24	43	56 %			

(actual / goal) x 100 = %

Running 6 day total
Day 1 _____ %
Day 2 __56__ %
Day 3 _____ %
Day 4 _____ %
Day 5 _____ %
Day 6 _____ %

Supporting Tasks	Complete
study mls	✓
post on facebook	✓

My Nightly Recap 🌙

Amount of Time wasted _____

🙂 What went right?

I woke up excited to reach out to others!

😣 What went wrong?

I did not have time to make the phone calls I had planned because of a family situation.

I am grateful for...

The ability to be flexible with my schedule.

Lead Generation notes:

Spoke with Steve. Their son is getting married. Need
to send a congrats card and follow up to see about
their housing needs.

Sally and Mike bought a house without me. I need to
keep up with them better, but they were glad I called
and they wished I had called sooner.

What scripts/dialog worked? (build on this)

loved the FSBO script I got from YouTube

What lead generating activities did I enjoy / not enjoy? Why?

I like the FORD technique. I'm not wild about
making phone calls, but they seem to be working.
I notice I get the best results between 9 - 11 in
actually reaching them.

What inspired me today? (if nothing, what will I do different tomorrow?)

I was mad at first that Mike and Sally bought w/o me
but it's inspired me to do a better job of reaching out
to potential buyers and sellers

Day 1

Date _____ △ _____ 🥤 _____

Hours available to work lead generation today _____

Activity	Actual	Goal	%	☺	😐	☹
Totals						

Running 6 day total
Day 1 %
Day 2 %
Day 3 %
Day 4 %
Day 5 %
Day 6 %

Supporting Tasks	Complete

My Nightly Recap 🌙

Amount of Time wasted _____

☺ What went right?

I am grateful for...

☹ What went wrong?

Lead Generation notes:

_____
_____
_____
_____
_____
_____
_____
_____
_____
_____
_____
_____

What scripts/dialog worked? (build on this)

_____
_____
_____
_____

What lead generating activities did I enjoy / not enjoy? Why?

_____
_____
_____
_____

What inspired me today? (if nothing, what will I do different tomorrow?)

_____
_____
_____
_____

Day 2

Date _____   🏕 _____   🥤 _____

Hours available to work lead generation today _____

Activity	Actual	Goal	%	☺	😐	☹		Running 6 day total	
								Day 1	%
								Day 2	%
								Day 3	%
								Day 4	%
Totals									

Supporting Tasks	Complete		Day 5	%
			Day 6	%

My Nightly Recap 🌙

Amount of Time wasted _____

☺ What went right?

I am grateful for...

☹ What went wrong?

Lead Generation notes:

_____

_____

_____

_____

_____

_____

_____

_____

_____

_____

_____

_____

_____

What scripts/dialog worked? (build on this)

_____

_____

_____

_____

What lead generating activities did I enjoy / not enjoy? Why?

_____

_____

_____

_____

What inspired me today? (if nothing, what will I do different tomorrow?)

_____

_____

_____

_____

Day 3

Date _____

Hours available to work lead generation today _____

Activity	Actual	Goal	%	😊	😐	☹️
Totals						

Supporting Tasks	Complete

Running 6 day total
Day 1 _____ %
Day 2 _____ %
Day 3 _____ %
Day 4 _____ %
Day 5 _____ %
Day 6 _____ %

My Nightly Recap

Amount of Time wasted _____

😊 What went right?

I am grateful for...

☹️ What went wrong?

Lead Generation notes:

_____

_____

_____

_____

_____

_____

_____

_____

_____

_____

_____

_____

What scripts/dialog worked? (build on this)

_____

_____

_____

_____

What lead generating activities did I enjoy / not enjoy? Why?

_____

_____

_____

_____

What inspired me today? (if nothing, what will I do different tomorrow?)

_____

_____

_____

_____

Day 4

Date _____ _____ _____

Hours available to work lead generation today _____

Activity	Actual	Goal	%	☺	😐	☹
Totals						

Running 6 day total
Day 1   %
Day 2   %
Day 3   %
Day 4   %
Day 5   %
Day 6   %

Supporting Tasks	Complete

My Nightly Recap 🌙

☺ What went right?

Amount of Time wasted _____

I am grateful for...

☹ What went wrong?

Lead Generation notes:

_____
_____
_____
_____
_____
_____
_____
_____
_____
_____
_____
_____

What scripts/dialog worked? (build on this)

_____
_____
_____
_____

What lead generating activities did I enjoy / not enjoy? Why?

_____
_____
_____
_____

What inspired me today? (if nothing, what will I do different tomorrow?)

_____
_____
_____
_____

Day 5

Date _____ 🏕 _____ 🥤 _____

Hours available to work lead generation today _____

Activity	Actual	Goal	%	🙂	😐	🙁
Totals						

Running 6 day total
Day 1 _____ %
Day 2 _____ %
Day 3 _____ %
Day 4 _____ %
Day 5 _____ %
Day 6 _____ %

Supporting Tasks	Complete

My Nightly Recap 🌙

Amount of Time wasted _____

🙂 What went right?

I am grateful for...

🙁 What went wrong?

Lead Generation notes:

_____
_____
_____
_____
_____
_____
_____
_____
_____
_____
_____
_____

What scripts/dialog worked? (build on this)

_____
_____
_____
_____

What lead generating activities did I enjoy / not enjoy? Why?

_____
_____
_____
_____

What inspired me today? (if nothing, what will I do different tomorrow?)

_____
_____
_____
_____

Day 6

Date _____   _____   _____

Hours available to work lead generation today _____

Activity	Actual	Goal	%	☺	😐	☹
Totals						

Running 6 day total

Day 1	%
Day 2	%
Day 3	%
Day 4	%
Day 5	%
Day 6	%

Supporting Tasks	Complete

My Nightly Recap

Amount of Time wasted _____

☺ What went right?

I am grateful for...

☹ What went wrong?

Lead Generation notes:

_____

_____

_____

_____

_____

_____

_____

_____

_____

_____

_____

_____

What scripts/dialog worked? (build on this)

_____

_____

_____

_____

What lead generating activities did I enjoy / not enjoy? Why?

_____

_____

_____

_____

What inspired me today? (if nothing, what will I do different tomorrow?)

_____

_____

_____

_____

LET'S GO ON AN
Adventure

Today is a rest day – a day to contemplate. Relax and let your creative side come out to play. Use these pages to jot down ideas and thoughts to help you grow your business. Have fun with it.

Grab your colored pencils! While you're coloring, think about things that don't serve you well.

Are there things you can let go of? Toss them in this fire.

Day 7

Date _____

Hours available to work lead generation today _____

Activity	Actual	Goal	%	☺	😐	☹
Totals						

Running 6 day total	
Day 1	%
Day 2	%
Day 3	%
Day 4	%
Day 5	%
Day 6	%

Supporting Tasks	Complete

My Nightly Recap

☺ What went right?

☹ What went wrong?

Amount of Time wasted _____

I am grateful for...

Lead Generation notes:

_____
_____
_____
_____
_____
_____
_____
_____
_____
_____
_____

What scripts/dialog worked? (build on this)

_____
_____
_____
_____

What lead generating activities did I enjoy / not enjoy? Why?

_____
_____
_____
_____

What inspired me today? (if nothing, what will I do different tomorrow?)

_____
_____
_____
_____
_____

Day 8

Date _____ ⛺ _____ 🥤 _____

Hours available to work lead generation today _____

Activity	Actual	Goal	%	🙂	😐	🙁
Totals						

Running 6 day total
Day 1 %
Day 2 %
Day 3 %
Day 4 %
Day 5 %
Day 6 %

Supporting Tasks	Complete

My Nightly Recap 🌙

🙂 What went right?

😟 What went wrong?

Amount of Time wasted _____

I am grateful for...

Lead Generation notes:

_____

_____

_____

_____

_____

_____

_____

_____

_____

_____

_____

_____

_____

What scripts/dialog worked? (build on this)

_____

_____

_____

_____

What lead generating activities did I enjoy / not enjoy? Why?

_____

_____

_____

_____

What inspired me today? (if nothing, what will I do different tomorrow?)

_____

_____

_____

_____

_____

Day 9

Date _____ ⛺ _____ 🥤 _____

Hours available to work lead generation today _____

Activity	Actual	Goal	%	🙂	😐	☹️
Totals						

Supporting Tasks	Complete

Running 6 day total	
Day 1	%
Day 2	%
Day 3	%
Day 4	%
Day 5	%
Day 6	%

My Nightly Recap 🌙

🙂 What went right?

☹️ What went wrong?

Amount of Time wasted _____

I am grateful for...

Lead Generation notes:

_____

_____

_____

_____

_____

_____

_____

_____

_____

_____

_____

_____

_____

What scripts/dialog worked? (build on this)

_____

_____

_____

_____

What lead generating activities did I enjoy / not enjoy? Why?

_____

_____

_____

_____

What inspired me today? (if nothing, what will I do different tomorrow?)

_____

_____

_____

_____

Day 10

Date _____ 🛖 _____ 🥤 _____

Hours available to work lead generation today _____

Activity	Actual	Goal	%	🙂	😐	☹️
Totals						

Running 6 day total	
Day 1	%
Day 2	%
Day 3	%
Day 4	%
Day 5	%
Day 6	%

Supporting Tasks	Complete

My Nightly Recap 🌙

Amount of Time wasted _____

🙂 What went right?

I am grateful for...

☹️ What went wrong?

Lead Generation notes:

_____

_____

_____

_____

_____

_____

_____

_____

_____

_____

_____

_____

_____

What scripts/dialog worked? (build on this)

_____

_____

_____

_____

What lead generating activities did I enjoy / not enjoy? Why?

_____

_____

_____

_____

What inspired me today? (if nothing, what will I do different tomorrow?)

_____

_____

_____

_____

Day 11

Date _____

Hours available to work lead generation today _____

Activity	Actual	Goal	%	☺	😐	☹
Totals						

Running 6 day total
Day 1 _____ %
Day 2 _____ %
Day 3 _____ %
Day 4 _____ %
Day 5 _____ %
Day 6 _____ %

Supporting Tasks	Complete

My Nightly Recap

Amount of Time wasted _____

☺ What went right?

I am grateful for...

☹ What went wrong?

Lead Generation notes:

_____

_____

_____

_____

_____

_____

_____

_____

_____

_____

_____

_____

What scripts/dialog worked? (build on this)

_____

_____

_____

_____

What lead generating activities did I enjoy / not enjoy? Why?

_____

_____

_____

_____

What inspired me today? (if nothing, what will I do different tomorrow?)

_____

_____

_____

_____

Day 12

Date _____ _____ _____

Hours available to work lead generation today _____

Activity	Actual	Goal	%	☺	😐	☹
Totals						

Running 6 day total
Day 1   %
Day 2   %
Day 3   %
Day 4   %
Day 5   %
Day 6   %

Supporting Tasks	Complete

My Nightly Recap 🌙

☺ What went right?

Amount of Time wasted _____

I am grateful for...

☹ What went wrong?

What went right over the last six days?

What went wrong over the last six days?

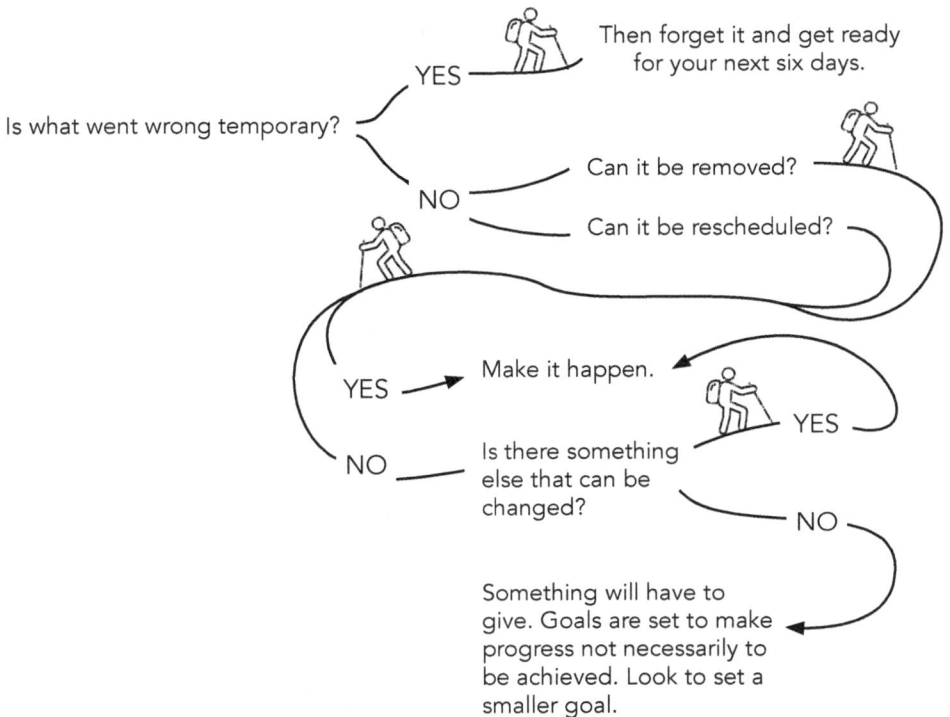

Is what went wrong temporary?

YES — Then forget it and get ready for your next six days.

NO — Can it be removed?

Can it be rescheduled?

YES → Make it happen.

YES

NO — Is there something else that can be changed?

NO

Something will have to give. Goals are set to make progress not necessarily to be achieved. Look to set a smaller goal.

Today is a rest day – a day to contemplate. Relax and let your creative side come out to play. Use these pages to jot down ideas and thoughts to help you grow your business. Have fun with it.

When it comes to real estate, who do I want around my campfire?

What do I enjoy about real estate?

Day 13

Date _____ ▲ _____ ☕ _____

Hours available to work lead generation today _____

Activity	Actual	Goal	%	☺	😐	☹
Totals						

Running 6 day total
Day 1   %
Day 2   %
Day 3   %
Day 4   %
Day 5   %
Day 6   %

Supporting Tasks	Complete

My Nightly Recap 🌙

☺ What went right?

☹ What went wrong?

Amount of Time wasted _____

I am grateful for...

Lead Generation notes:

_____

_____

_____

_____

_____

_____

_____

_____

_____

_____

_____

_____

What scripts/dialog worked? (build on this)

_____

_____

_____

_____

What lead generating activities did I enjoy / not enjoy? Why?

_____

_____

_____

_____

What inspired me today? (if nothing, what will I do different tomorrow?)

_____

_____

_____

_____

Day 14

Date _____

Hours available to work lead generation today _____

Activity	Actual	Goal	%	☺	😐	☹
Totals						

Supporting Tasks	Complete

Running 6 day total
Day 1 _____ %
Day 2 _____ %
Day 3 _____ %
Day 4 _____ %
Day 5 _____ %
Day 6 _____ %

My Nightly Recap

☺ What went right?

☹ What went wrong?

Amount of Time wasted _____

I am grateful for...

Lead Generation notes:

_____

_____

_____

_____

_____

_____

_____

_____

_____

_____

_____

What scripts/dialog worked? (build on this)

_____

_____

_____

_____

What lead generating activities did I enjoy / not enjoy? Why?

_____

_____

_____

_____

What inspired me today? (if nothing, what will I do different tomorrow?)

_____

_____

_____

_____

_____

Day 15

Date _____

Hours available to work lead generation today _____

Activity	Actual	Goal	%	😊	😐	😞
Totals						

Running 6 day total

Day 1	%
Day 2	%
Day 3	%
Day 4	%
Day 5	%
Day 6	%

Supporting Tasks	Complete

My Nightly Recap 🌙

😊 What went right?

😞 What went wrong?

Amount of Time wasted _____

I am grateful for...

Lead Generation notes:

_____
_____
_____
_____
_____
_____
_____
_____
_____
_____
_____
_____

What scripts/dialog worked? (build on this)

_____
_____
_____
_____

What lead generating activities did I enjoy / not enjoy? Why?

_____
_____
_____
_____

What inspired me today? (if nothing, what will I do different tomorrow?)

_____
_____
_____
_____

Day 16

Date _____ 🏕 _____ 🥤 _____

Hours available to work lead generation today _____

Activity	Actual	Goal	%	🙂	😐	☹️
Totals						

Running 6 day total

Day 1	%
Day 2	%
Day 3	%
Day 4	%
Day 5	%
Day 6	%

Supporting Tasks	Complete

My Nightly Recap 🌙

🙂 What went right?

😞 What went wrong?

Amount of Time wasted _____

I am grateful for...

Lead Generation notes:

_____
_____
_____
_____
_____
_____
_____
_____
_____
_____
_____
_____
_____

What scripts/dialog worked? (build on this)

_____
_____
_____
_____

What lead generating activities did I enjoy / not enjoy? Why?

_____
_____
_____
_____

What inspired me today? (if nothing, what will I do different tomorrow?)

_____
_____
_____
_____
_____

Day 17

Date _____

Hours available to work lead generation today _____

Activity	Actual	Goal	%	😊	😐	☹️
Totals						

Running 6 day total
Day 1 _____ %
Day 2 _____ %
Day 3 _____ %
Day 4 _____ %
Day 5 _____ %
Day 6 _____ %

Supporting Tasks	Complete

My Nightly Recap

😊 What went right?

😞 What went wrong?

Amount of Time wasted _____

I am grateful for...

Lead Generation notes:

_____

_____

_____

_____

_____

_____

_____

_____

_____

_____

_____

What scripts/dialog worked? (build on this)

_____

_____

_____

_____

What lead generating activities did I enjoy / not enjoy? Why?

_____

_____

_____

_____

What inspired me today? (if nothing, what will I do different tomorrow?)

_____

_____

_____

_____

_____

Day 18

Date _____ 🏕 _____ 🥤 _____

Hours available to work lead generation today _____

Activity	Actual	Goal	%	🙂	😐	☹		Running 6 day total
								Day 1 %
								Day 2 %
								Day 3 %
								Day 4 %
Totals								

Supporting Tasks	Complete		Day 5 %
			Day 6 %

My Nightly Recap 🌙

Amount of Time wasted _____

🙂 What went right?

I am grateful for...

☹ What went wrong?

What went right over the last six days?

What went wrong over the last six days?

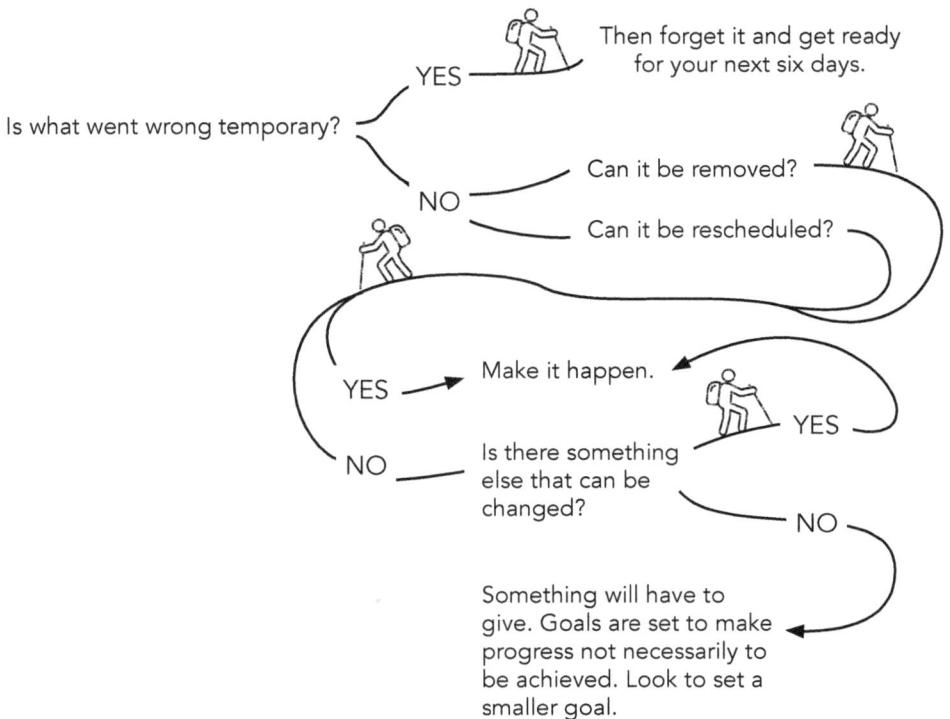

Is what went wrong temporary?

YES — Then forget it and get ready for your next six days.

NO — Can it be removed?

Can it be rescheduled?

YES → Make it happen.

NO — Is there something else that can be changed?

YES

NO

Something will have to give. Goals are set to make progress not necessarily to be achieved. Look to set a smaller goal.

Today is a rest day – a day to contemplate. Relax and let your creative side come out to play. Use these pages to jot down ideas and thoughts to help you grow your business. Have fun with it.

LET'S GO ON AN
Adventure

Give yourself a pep talk!

Day 19

Date _____

Hours available to work lead generation today _____

Activity	Actual	Goal	%	☺	😐	☹
Totals						

Supporting Tasks	Complete

Running 6 day total
Day 1 ____ %
Day 2 ____ %
Day 3 ____ %
Day 4 ____ %
Day 5 ____ %
Day 6 ____ %

My Nightly Recap

☺ What went right?

☹ What went wrong?

Amount of Time wasted _____

I am grateful for...

Lead Generation notes:

_____
_____
_____
_____
_____
_____
_____
_____
_____
_____
_____

What scripts/dialog worked? (build on this)

_____
_____
_____
_____

What lead generating activities did I enjoy / not enjoy? Why?

_____
_____
_____
_____

What inspired me today? (if nothing, what will I do different tomorrow?)

_____
_____
_____
_____

Day 20

Date _____ 🏕 _____ 🥤 _____

Hours available to work lead generation today _____

Activity	Actual	Goal	%	☺	😐	☹
Totals						

Running 6 day total
Day 1 __ %
Day 2 __ %
Day 3 __ %
Day 4 __ %
Day 5 __ %
Day 6 __ %

Supporting Tasks	Complete

My Nightly Recap 🌙

☺ What went right?

☹ What went wrong?

Amount of Time wasted _____

I am grateful for...

Lead Generation notes:

_____

_____

_____

_____

_____

_____

_____

_____

_____

_____

_____

_____

What scripts/dialog worked? (build on this)

_____

_____

_____

_____

What lead generating activities did I enjoy / not enjoy? Why?

_____

_____

_____

_____

What inspired me today? (if nothing, what will I do different tomorrow?)

_____

_____

_____

_____

Day 21

Date _____ 🏕 _____ 🥤 _____

Hours available to work lead generation today _____

Activity	Actual	Goal	%	🙂	😐	☹
Totals						

Supporting Tasks	Complete

Running 6 day total
Day 1
%
Day 2
%
Day 3
%
Day 4
%
Day 5
%
Day 6
%

My Nightly Recap 🌙

🙂 What went right?

😞 What went wrong?

Amount of Time wasted _____

I am grateful for...

Lead Generation notes:

_____

_____

_____

_____

_____

_____

_____

_____

_____

_____

_____

_____

_____

What scripts/dialog worked? (build on this)

_____

_____

_____

_____

What lead generating activities did I enjoy / not enjoy? Why?

_____

_____

_____

_____

What inspired me today? (if nothing, what will I do different tomorrow?)

_____

_____

_____

_____

Day 22

Date _____ 🏕 _____ 🥤 _____

Hours available to work lead generation today _____

Activity	Actual	Goal	%	🙂	😐	🙁
Totals						

Running 6 day total
Day 1   %
Day 2   %
Day 3   %
Day 4   %
Day 5   %
Day 6   %

Supporting Tasks	Complete

My Nightly Recap 🌙

🙂 What went right?

😟 What went wrong?

Amount of Time wasted _____

I am grateful for...

Lead Generation notes:

_____

_____

_____

_____

_____

_____

_____

_____

_____

_____

_____

_____

What scripts/dialog worked? (build on this)

_____

_____

_____

_____

What lead generating activities did I enjoy / not enjoy? Why?

_____

_____

_____

_____

What inspired me today? (if nothing, what will I do different tomorrow?)

_____

_____

_____

_____

Day 23

Date _____

Hours available to work lead generation today _____

Activity	Actual	Goal	%	☺	😐	☹
Totals						

Running 6 day total
Day 1 %
Day 2 %
Day 3 %
Day 4 %
Day 5 %
Day 6 %

Supporting Tasks	Complete

My Nightly Recap 🌙

Amount of Time wasted _____

☺ What went right?

I am grateful for...

☹ What went wrong?

Lead Generation notes:

_____
_____
_____
_____
_____
_____
_____
_____
_____
_____
_____
_____

What scripts/dialog worked? (build on this)

_____
_____
_____
_____

What lead generating activities did I enjoy / not enjoy? Why?

_____
_____
_____
_____

What inspired me today? (if nothing, what will I do different tomorrow?)

_____
_____
_____
_____

Day 24

Date _____ ⛺ _____ 🥤 _____

Hours available to work lead generation today _____

Activity	Actual	Goal	%	🙂	😐	🙁
Totals						

Running 6 day total
Day 1 %
Day 2 %
Day 3 %
Day 4 %
Day 5 %
Day 6 %

Supporting Tasks	Complete

My Nightly Recap 🌙

Amount of Time wasted _____

🙂 What went right?

I am grateful for...

🙁 What went wrong?

What went right over the last six days?

What went wrong over the last six days?

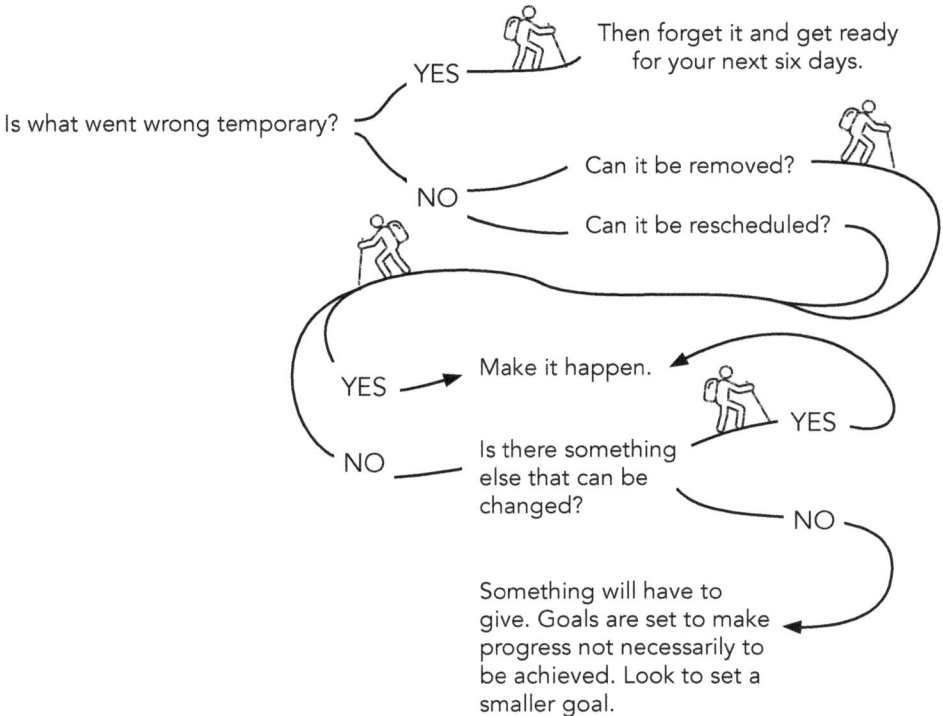

Is what went wrong temporary?

YES — Then forget it and get ready for your next six days.

NO — Can it be removed?

Can it be rescheduled?

YES → Make it happen.

YES

NO — Is there something else that can be changed?

NO

Something will have to give. Goals are set to make progress not necessarily to be achieved. Look to set a smaller goal.

Today is a rest day – a day to contemplate. Relax and let your creative side come out to play. Use these pages to jot down ideas and thoughts to help you grow your business. Have fun with it.

What is your biggest frustration in real estate right now?
And what will you do differently?

Day 25

Date _____ _____ _____

Hours available to work lead generation today _____

Activity	Actual	Goal	%	☺	😐	☹
Totals						

Running 6 day total
Day 1 %
Day 2 %
Day 3 %
Day 4 %
Day 5 %
Day 6 %

Supporting Tasks	Complete

My Nightly Recap 🌙

Amount of Time wasted _____

☺ What went right?

I am grateful for...

☹ What went wrong?

Lead Generation notes:

_____
_____
_____
_____
_____
_____
_____
_____
_____
_____
_____

What scripts/dialog worked? (build on this)

_____
_____
_____
_____

What lead generating activities did I enjoy / not enjoy? Why?

_____
_____
_____
_____

What inspired me today? (if nothing, what will I do different tomorrow?)

_____
_____
_____
_____

Day 26

Date _____

Hours available to work lead generation today _____

Activity	Actual	Goal	%	☺	😐	☹
Totals						

Running 6 day total
Day 1 _____ %
Day 2 _____ %
Day 3 _____ %
Day 4 _____ %
Day 5 _____ %
Day 6 _____ %

Supporting Tasks	Complete

My Nightly Recap

Amount of Time wasted _____

☺ What went right?

I am grateful for...

☹ What went wrong?

Lead Generation notes:

_____
_____
_____
_____
_____
_____
_____
_____
_____
_____
_____

What scripts/dialog worked? (build on this)

_____
_____
_____
_____

What lead generating activities did I enjoy / not enjoy? Why?

_____
_____
_____
_____

What inspired me today? (if nothing, what will I do different tomorrow?)

_____
_____
_____
_____

Day 27

Date _____

Hours available to work lead generation today _____

Activity	Actual	Goal	%	😊	😐	😞
Totals						

Supporting Tasks	Complete

Running 6 day total
Day 1
%
Day 2
%
Day 3
%
Day 4
%
Day 5
%
Day 6
%

My Nightly Recap

Amount of Time wasted _____

😊 What went right?

I am grateful for...

😞 What went wrong?

Lead Generation notes:

_____

_____

_____

_____

_____

_____

_____

_____

_____

_____

_____

_____

What scripts/dialog worked? (build on this)

_____

_____

_____

_____

What lead generating activities did I enjoy / not enjoy? Why?

_____

_____

_____

_____

What inspired me today? (if nothing, what will I do different tomorrow?)

_____

_____

_____

_____

Day 28

Date _____ 🏕 _____ 🥤 _____

Hours available to work lead generation today _____

Activity	Actual	Goal	%	🙂	😐	🙁		Running 6 day total	
								Day 1	%
								Day 2	%
								Day 3	%
								Day 4	%
Totals									

Supporting Tasks	Complete		Day 5	%
			Day 6	%

My Nightly Recap 🌙

🙂 What went right?

Amount of Time wasted _____

I am grateful for...

🙁 What went wrong?

Lead Generation notes:

_____

_____

_____

_____

_____

_____

_____

_____

_____

_____

_____

_____

_____

What scripts/dialog worked? (build on this)

_____

_____

_____

_____

What lead generating activities did I enjoy / not enjoy? Why?

_____

_____

_____

_____

What inspired me today? (if nothing, what will I do different tomorrow?)

_____

_____

_____

_____

Day 29

Date _____ 🏕 _____ 🥤 _____

Hours available to work lead generation today _____

Activity	Actual	Goal	%	😊	😐	😞
Totals						

Running 6 day total
Day 1   %
Day 2   %
Day 3   %
Day 4   %
Day 5   %
Day 6   %

Supporting Tasks	Complete

My Nightly Recap 🌙

😊 What went right?

😞 What went wrong?

Amount of Time wasted _____

I am grateful for...

Lead Generation notes:

_____
_____
_____
_____
_____
_____
_____
_____
_____
_____
_____
_____
_____
_____

What scripts/dialog worked? (build on this)

_____
_____
_____
_____
_____

What lead generating activities did I enjoy / not enjoy? Why?

_____
_____
_____
_____
_____

What inspired me today? (if nothing, what will I do different tomorrow?)

_____
_____
_____
_____
_____

Day 30

Date _____

Hours available to work lead generation today _____

Activity	Actual	Goal	%	🙂	😐	🙁
Totals						

Supporting Tasks	Complete

Running 6 day total

Day 1	%
Day 2	%
Day 3	%
Day 4	%
Day 5	%
Day 6	%

My Nightly Recap

🙂 What went right?

🙁 What went wrong?

Amount of Time wasted _____

I am grateful for...

What went right over the last six days?

What went wrong over the last six days?

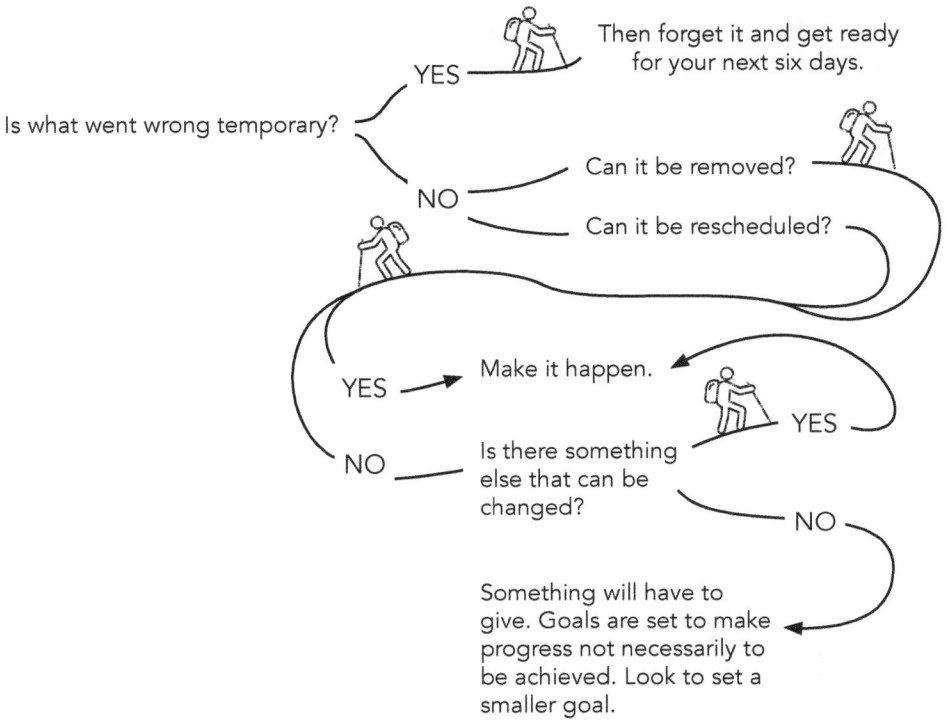

Is what went wrong temporary?

YES — Then forget it and get ready for your next six days.

NO — Can it be removed?

Can it be rescheduled?

YES → Make it happen.

NO — Is there something else that can be changed?

YES

NO

Something will have to give. Goals are set to make progress not necessarily to be achieved. Look to set a smaller goal.

LET'S GO ON AN
Adventure

Today is a rest day – a day to contemplate. Relax and let your creative side come out to play. Use these pages to jot down ideas and thoughts to help you grow your business. Have fun with it.

What direction do you want to go in? First time home buyers? Luxury Living? Something in between? Jot it down here.

Day 31

Date _____ 🏕 _____ 🥤 _____

Hours available to work lead generation today _____

Activity	Actual	Goal	%	☺	😐	☹
Totals						

Running 6 day total
Day 1 %
Day 2 %
Day 3 %
Day 4 %
Day 5 %
Day 6 %

Supporting Tasks	Complete

My Nightly Recap 🌙

Amount of Time wasted _____

☺ What went right?

I am grateful for...

☹ What went wrong?

Lead Generation notes:

_____
_____
_____
_____
_____
_____
_____
_____
_____
_____
_____
_____

What scripts/dialog worked? (build on this)

_____
_____
_____
_____

What lead generating activities did I enjoy / not enjoy? Why?

_____
_____
_____
_____

What inspired me today? (if nothing, what will I do different tomorrow?)

_____
_____
_____
_____
_____

Day 32

Date _____

Hours available to work lead generation today _____

Activity	Actual	Goal	%	☺	😐	☹
Totals						

Running 6 day total
Day 1 %
Day 2 %
Day 3 %
Day 4 %
Day 5 %
Day 6 %

Supporting Tasks	Complete

My Nightly Recap

☺ What went right?

☹ What went wrong?

Amount of Time wasted _____

I am grateful for...

Lead Generation notes:

_____

_____

_____

_____

_____

_____

_____

_____

_____

_____

_____

_____

What scripts/dialog worked? (build on this)

_____

_____

_____

_____

What lead generating activities did I enjoy / not enjoy? Why?

_____

_____

_____

_____

What inspired me today? (if nothing, what will I do different tomorrow?)

_____

_____

_____

_____

Day 33

Date _____ 🏕 _____ 🥤 _____

Hours available to work lead generation today _____

Activity	Actual	Goal	%	☺	😐	☹		Running 6 day total
								Day 1
								%
								Day 2
								%
								Day 3
								%
Totals								Day 4
								%

Supporting Tasks	Complete		Day 5
			%
			Day 6
			%

My Nightly Recap 🌙

☺ What went right?

Amount of Time wasted _____

I am grateful for...

☹ What went wrong?

Lead Generation notes:

_____

_____

_____

_____

_____

_____

_____

_____

_____

_____

_____

What scripts/dialog worked? (build on this)

_____

_____

_____

_____

What lead generating activities did I enjoy / not enjoy? Why?

_____

_____

_____

_____

What inspired me today? (if nothing, what will I do different tomorrow?)

_____

_____

_____

_____

Day 34

Date _____   🏕 _____   🥤 _____

Hours available to work lead generation today _____

Activity	Actual	Goal	%	🙂	😐	🙁	Running 6 day total
							Day 1
							%
							Day 2
							%
							Day 3
							%
							Day 4
							%
Totals							
							Day 5

Supporting Tasks	Complete	
		Day 5
		%
		Day 6
		%

My Nightly Recap 🌙

🙂 What went right?

🙁 What went wrong?

Amount of Time wasted _____

I am grateful for...

Lead Generation notes:

_____

_____

_____

_____

_____

_____

_____

_____

_____

_____

_____

_____

What scripts/dialog worked? (build on this)

_____

_____

_____

_____

What lead generating activities did I enjoy / not enjoy? Why?

_____

_____

_____

_____

What inspired me today? (if nothing, what will I do different tomorrow?)

_____

_____

_____

_____

Day 35

Date _____ ⛺ _____ 🥤 _____

Hours available to work lead generation today _____

Activity	Actual	Goal	%	☺	😐	☹
Totals						

Supporting Tasks	Complete

Running 6 day total
Day 1 %
Day 2 %
Day 3 %
Day 4 %
Day 5 %
Day 6 %

My Nightly Recap 🌙

☺ What went right?

☹ What went wrong?

Amount of Time wasted _____

I am grateful for...

Lead Generation notes:

_____

_____

_____

_____

_____

_____

_____

_____

_____

_____

_____

_____

What scripts/dialog worked? (build on this)

_____

_____

_____

_____

What lead generating activities did I enjoy / not enjoy? Why?

_____

_____

_____

_____

What inspired me today? (if nothing, what will I do different tomorrow?)

_____

_____

_____

_____

Day 36

Date _____ 🏕 _____ 🥤 _____

Hours available to work lead generation today _____

Activity	Actual	Goal	%	🙂	😐	☹️
Totals						

Running 6 day total
Day 1 %
Day 2 %
Day 3 %
Day 4 %
Day 5 %
Day 6 %

Supporting Tasks	Complete

My Nightly Recap 🌙

🙂 What went right?

😞 What went wrong?

Amount of Time wasted _____

I am grateful for...

What went right over the last six days?

What went wrong over the last six days?

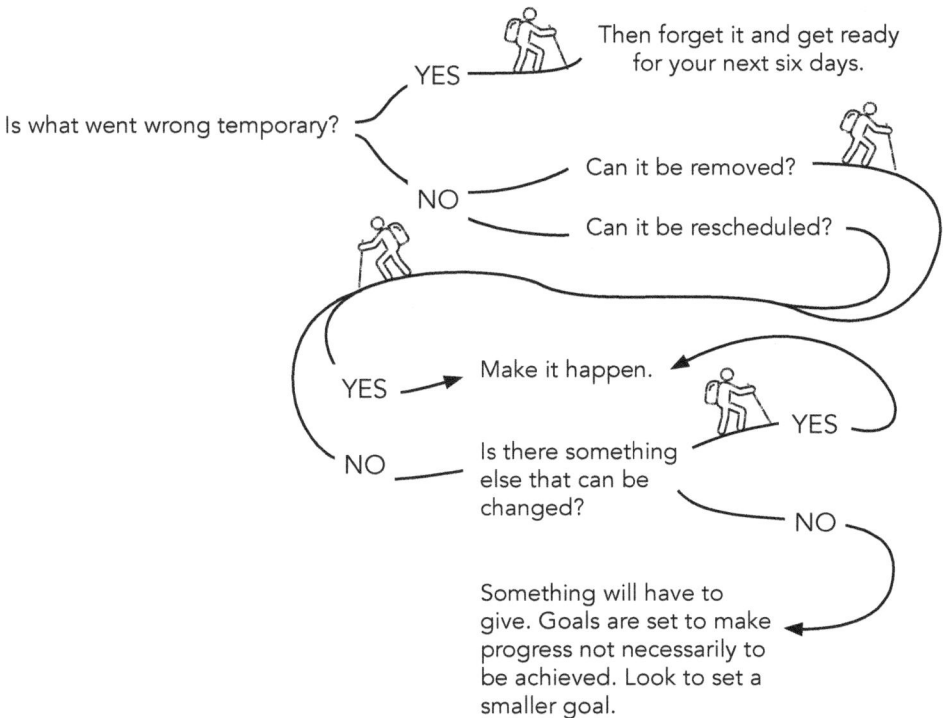

Is what went wrong temporary?

YES — Then forget it and get ready for your next six days.

NO —

Can it be removed?

Can it be rescheduled?

YES → Make it happen.

YES

NO — Is there something else that can be changed?

NO

Something will have to give. Goals are set to make progress not necessarily to be achieved. Look to set a smaller goal.

Today is a rest day – a day to contemplate. Relax and let your creative side come out to play. Use these pages to jot down ideas and thoughts to help you grow your business. Have fun with it.

What techniques have you
found to be most effective
in capturing leads?

Date _____ _____ _____

Hours available to work lead generation today _____

Activity	Actual	Goal	%	☺	😐	☹
Totals						

Running 6 day total
Day 1 ____ %
Day 2 ____ %
Day 3 ____ %
Day 4 ____ %
Day 5 ____ %
Day 6 ____ %

Supporting Tasks	Complete

My Nightly Recap

☺ What went right?

☹ What went wrong?

Amount of Time wasted _____

I am grateful for...

Lead Generation notes:

_____

_____

_____

_____

_____

_____

_____

_____

_____

_____

_____

_____

What scripts/dialog worked? (build on this)

_____

_____

_____

_____

What lead generating activities did I enjoy / not enjoy? Why?

_____

_____

_____

_____

What inspired me today? (if nothing, what will I do different tomorrow?)

_____

_____

_____

_____

Day 38

Date _____

Hours available to work lead generation today _____

Activity	Actual	Goal	%	☺	😐	☹
Totals						

Supporting Tasks	Complete

Running 6 day total
Day 1 %
Day 2 %
Day 3 %
Day 4 %
Day 5 %
Day 6 %

My Nightly Recap

☺ What went right?

☹ What went wrong?

Amount of Time wasted _____

I am grateful for...

Lead Generation notes:

_____
_____
_____
_____
_____
_____
_____
_____
_____
_____
_____
_____
_____

What scripts/dialog worked? (build on this)

_____
_____
_____
_____

What lead generating activities did I enjoy / not enjoy? Why?

_____
_____
_____
_____

What inspired me today? (if nothing, what will I do different tomorrow?)

_____
_____
_____
_____

Day 39

Date _____

Hours available to work lead generation today _____

Activity	Actual	Goal	%	☺	😐	☹
Totals						

Running 6 day total
Day 1 _____ %
Day 2 _____ %
Day 3 _____ %
Day 4 _____ %
Day 5 _____ %
Day 6 _____ %

Supporting Tasks	Complete

My Nightly Recap

☺ What went right?

☹ What went wrong?

Amount of Time wasted _____

I am grateful for...

Lead Generation notes:

_____

_____

_____

_____

_____

_____

_____

_____

_____

_____

_____

_____

What scripts/dialog worked? (build on this)

_____

_____

_____

_____

What lead generating activities did I enjoy / not enjoy? Why?

_____

_____

_____

_____

What inspired me today? (if nothing, what will I do different tomorrow?)

_____

_____

_____

_____

Day 40

Date _____

Hours available to work lead generation today _____

Activity	Actual	Goal	%	☺	😐	☹
Totals						

Running 6 day total
Day 1 %
Day 2 %
Day 3 %
Day 4 %
Day 5 %
Day 6 %

Supporting Tasks	Complete

My Nightly Recap

☺ What went right?

☹ What went wrong?

Amount of Time wasted _____

I am grateful for...

Lead Generation notes:

_____
_____
_____
_____
_____
_____
_____
_____
_____
_____
_____
_____
_____

What scripts/dialog worked? (build on this)

_____
_____
_____
_____

What lead generating activities did I enjoy / not enjoy? Why?

_____
_____
_____
_____

What inspired me today? (if nothing, what will I do different tomorrow?)

_____
_____
_____
_____

Day 41

Date _____

Hours available to work lead generation today _____

Activity	Actual	Goal	%	☺	😐	☹
Totals						

Running 6 day total
Day 1 %
Day 2 %
Day 3 %
Day 4 %
Day 5 %
Day 6 %

Supporting Tasks	Complete

My Nightly Recap

Amount of Time wasted _____

☺ What went right?

I am grateful for...

☹ What went wrong?

Lead Generation notes:

_____
_____
_____
_____
_____
_____
_____
_____
_____
_____
_____
_____

What scripts/dialog worked? (build on this)

_____
_____
_____
_____

What lead generating activities did I enjoy / not enjoy? Why?

_____
_____
_____
_____

What inspired me today? (if nothing, what will I do different tomorrow?)

_____
_____
_____
_____

Day 42

Date _____

Hours available to work lead generation today _____

Activity	Actual	Goal	%	☺	😐	☹
Totals						

Running 6 day total
Day 1 __ %
Day 2 __ %
Day 3 __ %
Day 4 __ %
Day 5 __ %
Day 6 __ %

Supporting Tasks	Complete

My Nightly Recap

Amount of Time wasted _____

☺ What went right?

I am grateful for...

☹ What went wrong?

What went right over the last six days?

What went wrong over the last six days?

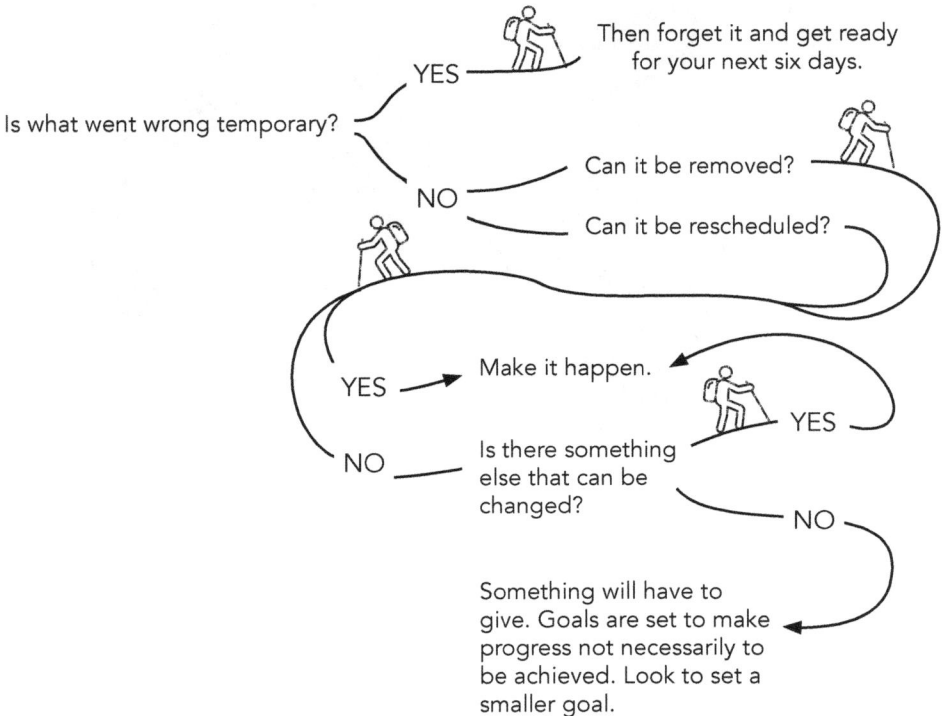

Is what went wrong temporary?

YES — Then forget it and get ready for your next six days.

NO

Can it be removed?

Can it be rescheduled?

YES → Make it happen.

NO — Is there something else that can be changed?

YES

NO

Something will have to give. Goals are set to make progress not necessarily to be achieved. Look to set a smaller goal.

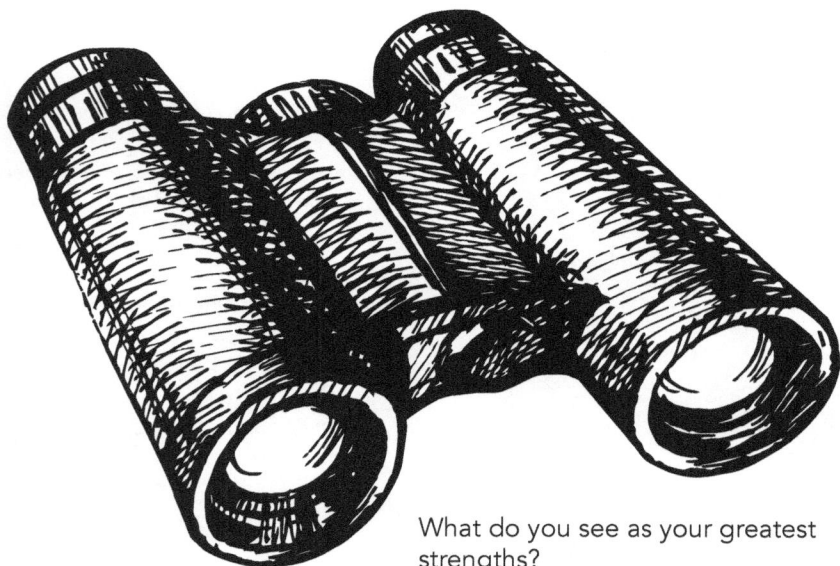
LET'S GO ON AN
Adventure

Today is a rest day – a day to contemplate. Relax and let your creative side come out to play. Use these pages to jot down ideas and thoughts to help you grow your business. Have fun with it.

What do you see as your greatest strengths?

List them:

Day 43

Date _____

Hours available to work lead generation today _____

Activity	Actual	Goal	%	☺	😐	☹
Totals						

Running 6 day total
Day 1 %
Day 2 %
Day 3 %
Day 4 %
Day 5 %
Day 6 %

Supporting Tasks	Complete

My Nightly Recap

☺ What went right?

☹ What went wrong?

Amount of Time wasted _____

I am grateful for...

Lead Generation notes:

_____
_____
_____
_____
_____
_____
_____
_____
_____
_____
_____

What scripts/dialog worked? (build on this)

_____
_____
_____
_____

What lead generating activities did I enjoy / not enjoy? Why?

_____
_____
_____
_____

What inspired me today? (if nothing, what will I do different tomorrow?)

_____
_____
_____
_____
_____

Day 44

Date _____

Hours available to work lead generation today _____

Activity	Actual	Goal	%	☺	😐	☹		Running 6 day total
								Day 1 %
								Day 2 %
								Day 3 %
								Day 4 %
Totals								
								Day 5 %

Supporting Tasks	Complete

Day 6 %

My Nightly Recap 🌙

Amount of Time wasted _____

☺ What went right?

I am grateful for...

☹ What went wrong?

Lead Generation notes:

_____
_____
_____
_____
_____
_____
_____
_____
_____
_____
_____
_____

What scripts/dialog worked? (build on this)

_____
_____
_____
_____

What lead generating activities did I enjoy / not enjoy? Why?

_____
_____
_____
_____

What inspired me today? (if nothing, what will I do different tomorrow?)

_____
_____
_____
_____

Day 45

Date _____ ⛺ _____ 🥤 _____

Hours available to work lead generation today _____

Activity	Actual	Goal	%	🙂	😐	🙁
Totals						

Running 6 day total
Day 1   %
Day 2   %
Day 3   %
Day 4   %
Day 5   %
Day 6   %

Supporting Tasks	Complete

My Nightly Recap 🌙

Amount of Time wasted _____

🙂 What went right?

I am grateful for...

🙁 What went wrong?

Lead Generation notes:

_____

_____

_____

_____

_____

_____

_____

_____

_____

_____

_____

_____

_____

What scripts/dialog worked? (build on this)

_____

_____

_____

_____

What lead generating activities did I enjoy / not enjoy? Why?

_____

_____

_____

_____

What inspired me today? (if nothing, what will I do different tomorrow?)

_____

_____

_____

_____

Day 46

Date _____ ⛺ _____ 🥤 _____

Hours available to work lead generation today _____

Activity	Actual	Goal	%	☺	😐	☹
Totals						

Running 6 day total	
Day 1	%
Day 2	%
Day 3	%
Day 4	%
Day 5	%
Day 6	%

Supporting Tasks	Complete

My Nightly Recap 🌙

☺ What went right?

Amount of Time wasted _____

I am grateful for...

☹ What went wrong?

Lead Generation notes:

_____

_____

_____

_____

_____

_____

_____

_____

_____

_____

_____

_____

What scripts/dialog worked? (build on this)

_____

_____

_____

_____

What lead generating activities did I enjoy / not enjoy? Why?

_____

_____

_____

_____

What inspired me today? (if nothing, what will I do different tomorrow?)

_____

_____

_____

_____

_____

Day 47

Hours available to work lead generation today _____

Activity	Actual	Goal	%	😊	😐	☹️
Totals						

Supporting Tasks	Complete

Running 6 day total

Day 1 _____ %

Day 2 _____ %

Day 3 _____ %

Day 4 _____ %

Day 5 _____ %

Day 6 _____ %

My Nightly Recap

😊 What went right?

☹️ What went wrong?

Amount of Time wasted _____

I am grateful for...

Lead Generation notes:

_____
_____
_____
_____
_____
_____
_____
_____
_____
_____
_____
_____

What scripts/dialog worked? (build on this)

_____
_____
_____
_____

What lead generating activities did I enjoy / not enjoy? Why?

_____
_____
_____
_____

What inspired me today? (if nothing, what will I do different tomorrow?)

_____
_____
_____
_____
_____

Day 48

Date _____

Hours available to work lead generation today _____

Activity	Actual	Goal	%	☺	😐	☹
Totals						

Running 6 day total
Day 1 %
Day 2 %
Day 3 %
Day 4 %
Day 5 %
Day 6 %

Supporting Tasks	Complete

My Nightly Recap

Amount of Time wasted _____

☺ What went right?

I am grateful for...

☹ What went wrong?

What went right over the last six days?

What went wrong over the last six days?

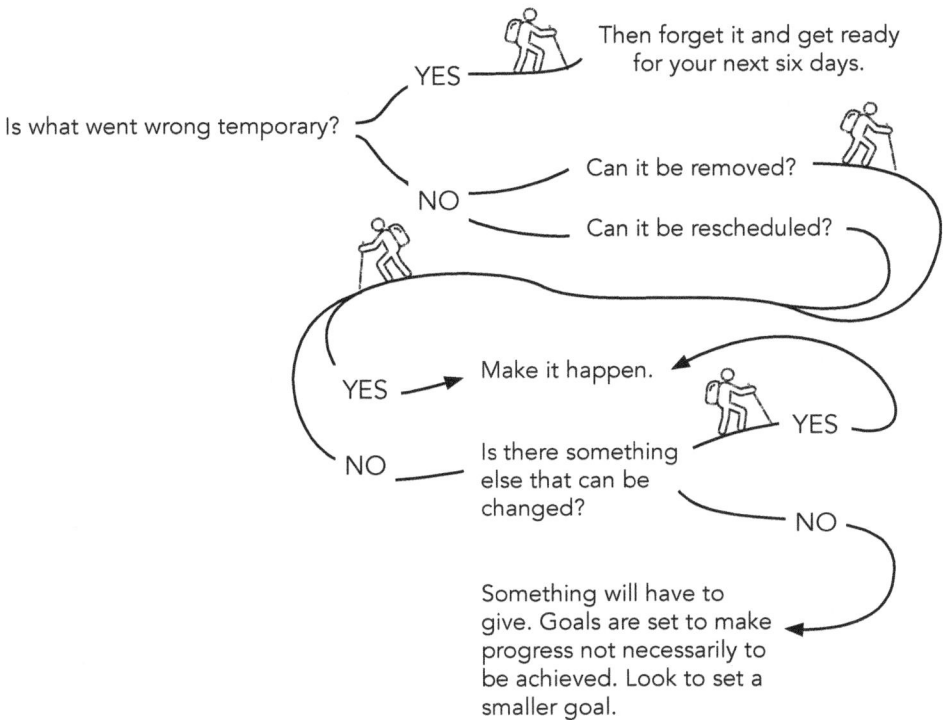

YES — Then forget it and get ready
for your next six days.

Is what went wrong temporary?

Can it be removed?

NO

Can it be rescheduled?

YES → Make it happen.

NO — Is there something
else that can be
changed?

YES

NO

Something will have to
give. Goals are set to make
progress not necessarily to
be achieved. Look to set a
smaller goal.

Today is a rest day – a day to contemplate. Relax and let your creative side come out to play. Use these pages to jot down ideas and thoughts to help you grow your business. Have fun with it.

Enjoy this day!

Day 49

Date _____ 🏕 _____ 🥤 _____

Hours available to work lead generation today _____

Activity	Actual	Goal	%	☺	😐	☹
Totals						

Running 6 day total
Day 1   %
Day 2   %
Day 3   %
Day 4   %
Day 5   %
Day 6   %

Supporting Tasks	Complete

My Nightly Recap 🌙

☺ What went right?

☹ What went wrong?

Amount of Time wasted _____

I am grateful for...

Lead Generation notes:

_____

_____

_____

_____

_____

_____

_____

_____

_____

_____

_____

_____

_____

What scripts/dialog worked? (build on this)

_____

_____

_____

_____

What lead generating activities did I enjoy / not enjoy? Why?

_____

_____

_____

_____

What inspired me today? (if nothing, what will I do different tomorrow?)

_____

_____

_____

_____

_____

Day 50

Date _____ 🏕 _____ 🥤 _____

Hours available to work lead generation today _____

Activity	Actual	Goal	%	🙂	😐	🙁
Totals						

Running 6 day total
Day 1 ____%
Day 2 ____%
Day 3 ____%
Day 4 ____%
Day 5 ____%
Day 6 ____%

Supporting Tasks	Complete

My Nightly Recap 🌙

🙂 What went right?

😟 What went wrong?

Amount of Time wasted _____

I am grateful for...

Lead Generation notes:

_____
_____
_____
_____
_____
_____
_____
_____
_____
_____
_____
_____

What scripts/dialog worked? (build on this)

_____
_____
_____
_____

What lead generating activities did I enjoy / not enjoy? Why?

_____
_____
_____
_____

What inspired me today? (if nothing, what will I do different tomorrow?)

_____
_____
_____
_____

Day 51

Date _____ 🏕 _____ 🥤 _____

Hours available to work lead generation today _____

Activity	Actual	Goal	%	🙂	😐	🙁		Running 6 day total
								Day 1
								%
								Day 2
								%
								Day 3
								%
								Day 4
Totals								%

Supporting Tasks	Complete		Day 5
			%
			Day 6
			%

My Nightly Recap 🌙

🙂 What went right?

Amount of Time wasted _____

I am grateful for...

🙁 What went wrong?

Lead Generation notes:

_____

_____

_____

_____

_____

_____

_____

_____

_____

_____

_____

_____

What scripts/dialog worked? (build on this)

_____

_____

_____

_____

What lead generating activities did I enjoy / not enjoy? Why?

_____

_____

_____

_____

What inspired me today? (if nothing, what will I do different tomorrow?)

_____

_____

_____

_____

Day 52

Date _____   🏕️ _____   🥤 _____

Hours available to work lead generation today _____

Activity	Actual	Goal	%	☺	😐	☹
Totals						

Running 6 day total

Day 1	%
Day 2	%
Day 3	%
Day 4	%
Day 5	%
Day 6	%

Supporting Tasks	Complete

My Nightly Recap 🌙

Amount of Time wasted _____

☺ What went right?

I am grateful for...

☹ What went wrong?

Lead Generation notes:

_____

_____

_____

_____

_____

_____

_____

_____

_____

_____

_____

_____

_____

What scripts/dialog worked? (build on this)

_____

_____

_____

_____

_____

What lead generating activities did I enjoy / not enjoy? Why?

_____

_____

_____

_____

_____

What inspired me today? (if nothing, what will I do different tomorrow?)

_____

_____

_____

_____

_____

Day 53

Date _____

Hours available to work lead generation today _____

Activity	Actual	Goal	%	☺	😐	☹
Totals						

Running 6 day total
Day 1 ___%
Day 2 ___%
Day 3 ___%
Day 4 ___%
Day 5 ___%
Day 6 ___%

Supporting Tasks	Complete

My Nightly Recap

Amount of Time wasted _____

☺ What went right?

I am grateful for...

☹ What went wrong?

Lead Generation notes:

_____

_____

_____

_____

_____

_____

_____

_____

_____

_____

_____

_____

_____

What scripts/dialog worked? (build on this)

_____

_____

_____

_____

What lead generating activities did I enjoy / not enjoy? Why?

_____

_____

_____

_____

What inspired me today? (if nothing, what will I do different tomorrow?)

_____

_____

_____

_____

Day 54

Date _____   🏕 _____   🥤 _____

Hours available to work lead generation today _____

Activity	Actual	Goal	%	😊	😐	☹️		Running 6 day total
								Day 1
								%
								Day 2
								%
								Day 3
								%
Totals								**Day 4**
								%

Supporting Tasks	Complete		Running 6 day total
			Day 5
			%
			Day 6
			%

My Nightly Recap 🌙

😊 What went right?

☹️ What went wrong?

Amount of Time wasted _____

I am grateful for...

What went right over the last six days?

What went wrong over the last six days?

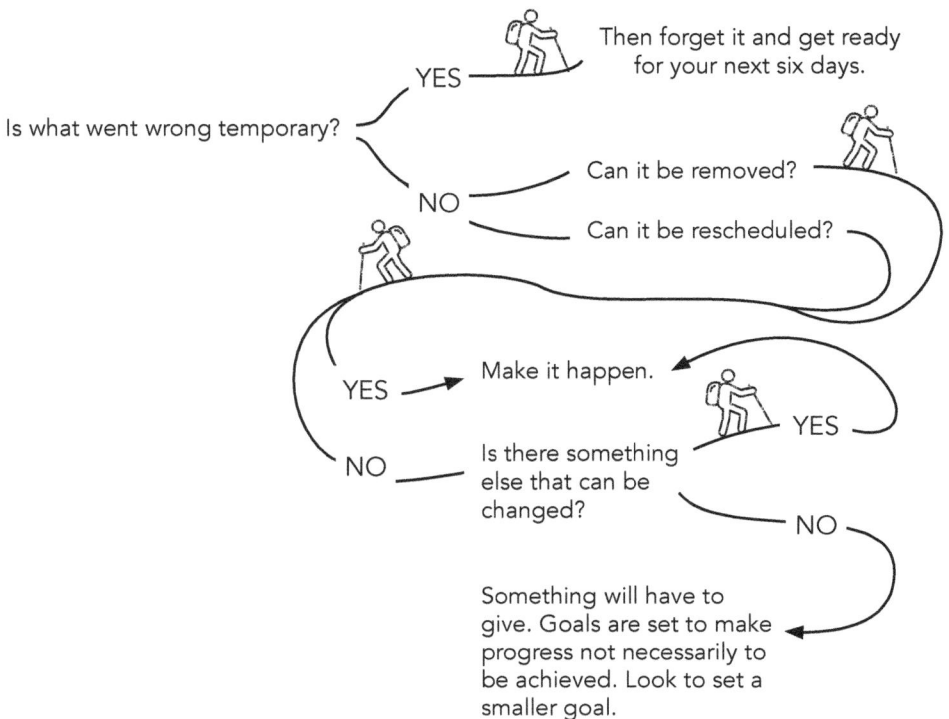

Is what went wrong temporary?

YES — Then forget it and get ready for your next six days.

NO

Can it be removed?

Can it be rescheduled?

YES → Make it happen.

NO — Is there something else that can be changed?

YES

NO

Something will have to give. Goals are set to make progress not necessarily to be achieved. Look to set a smaller goal.

Today is a rest day – a day to contemplate. Relax and let your creative side come out to play. Use these pages to jot down ideas and thoughts to help you grow your business. Have fun with it.

LET'S GO ON AN
Adventure

What do you need to put in your real estate backpack? More education? New computer? A designation?

Day 55

Date _____

Hours available to work lead generation today _____

Activity	Actual	Goal	%	☺	😐	☹
Totals						

Supporting Tasks	Complete

Running 6 day total
Day 1 _____ %
Day 2 _____ %
Day 3 _____ %
Day 4 _____ %
Day 5 _____ %
Day 6 _____ %

My Nightly Recap

Amount of Time wasted _____

☺ What went right?

I am grateful for...

☹ What went wrong?

Lead Generation notes:

_____
_____
_____
_____
_____
_____
_____
_____
_____
_____
_____

What scripts/dialog worked? (build on this)

_____
_____
_____
_____

What lead generating activities did I enjoy / not enjoy? Why?

_____
_____
_____
_____

What inspired me today? (if nothing, what will I do different tomorrow?)

_____
_____
_____
_____
_____

Day 56

Date _____

Hours available to work lead generation today _____

Activity	Actual	Goal	%	☺	😐	☹
Totals						

Running 6 day total
Day 1 __%
Day 2 __%
Day 3 __%
Day 4 __%
Day 5 __%
Day 6 __%

Supporting Tasks	Complete

My Nightly Recap

Amount of Time wasted _____

☺ What went right?

I am grateful for...

☹ What went wrong?

Lead Generation notes:

_____
_____
_____
_____
_____
_____
_____
_____
_____
_____
_____
_____

What scripts/dialog worked? (build on this)

_____
_____
_____
_____

What lead generating activities did I enjoy / not enjoy? Why?

_____
_____
_____
_____

What inspired me today? (if nothing, what will I do different tomorrow?)

_____
_____
_____
_____

Day 57

Date _____ 🏕 _____ 🥤 _____

Hours available to work lead generation today _____

Activity	Actual	Goal	%	☺	😐	☹
Totals						

Supporting Tasks	Complete

Running 6 day total

Day 1	%
Day 2	%
Day 3	%
Day 4	%
Day 5	%
Day 6	%

My Nightly Recap 🌙

Amount of Time wasted _____

☺ What went right?

I am grateful for...

☹ What went wrong?

Lead Generation notes:

_____

_____

_____

_____

_____

_____

_____

_____

_____

_____

_____

_____

What scripts/dialog worked? (build on this)

_____

_____

_____

_____

What lead generating activities did I enjoy / not enjoy? Why?

_____

_____

_____

_____

What inspired me today? (if nothing, what will I do different tomorrow?)

_____

_____

_____

_____

Day 58

Date _____ 🏕 _____ 🥤 _____

Hours available to work lead generation today _____

Activity	Actual	Goal	%	☺	😐	☹
Totals						

Running 6 day total
Day 1 ____ %
Day 2 ____ %
Day 3 ____ %
Day 4 ____ %
Day 5 ____ %
Day 6 ____ %

Supporting Tasks	Complete

My Nightly Recap 🌙

Amount of Time wasted _____

☺ What went right?

I am grateful for...

☹ What went wrong?

Lead Generation notes:

What scripts/dialog worked? (build on this)

What lead generating activities did I enjoy / not enjoy? Why?

What inspired me today? (if nothing, what will I do different tomorrow?)

Day 59

Date _____

Hours available to work lead generation today _____

Activity	Actual	Goal	%	☺	😐	☹
Totals						

Running 6 day total
Day 1 %
Day 2 %
Day 3 %
Day 4 %
Day 5 %
Day 6 %

Supporting Tasks	Complete

My Nightly Recap 🌙

Amount of Time wasted _____

☺ What went right?

I am grateful for...

☹ What went wrong?

Lead Generation notes:

_____

_____

_____

_____

_____

_____

_____

_____

_____

_____

_____

_____

_____

What scripts/dialog worked? (build on this)

_____

_____

_____

_____

What lead generating activities did I enjoy / not enjoy? Why?

_____

_____

_____

_____

What inspired me today? (if nothing, what will I do different tomorrow?)

_____

_____

_____

_____

_____

Day 60

Date _____   🏕 _____   🥤 _____

Hours available to work lead generation today _____

Activity	Actual	Goal	%	☺	😐	☹
Totals						

Running 6 day total
Day 1 %
Day 2 %
Day 3 %
Day 4 %
Day 5 %
Day 6 %

Supporting Tasks	Complete

My Nightly Recap 🌙

Amount of Time wasted _____

☺ What went right?

I am grateful for...

☹ What went wrong?

Lead Generation notes:

_____
_____
_____
_____
_____
_____
_____
_____
_____
_____
_____
_____

What scripts/dialog worked? (build on this)

_____
_____
_____
_____

What lead generating activities did I enjoy / not enjoy? Why?

_____
_____
_____
_____

What inspired me today? (if nothing, what will I do different tomorrow?)

_____
_____
_____
_____

Today is a rest day – a day to contemplate. Relax and let your creative side come out to play. Use these pages to jot down ideas and thoughts to help you grow your business. Have fun with it.

What kind of market have
you discovered you like
working in?

Day 61

Date _____ 🏕 _____ 🥤 _____

Hours available to work lead generation today _____

Activity	Actual	Goal	%	🙂	😐	☹	Running 6 day total
							Day 1 %
							Day 2 %
							Day 3 %
							Day 4 %
Totals							

Supporting Tasks	Complete	
		Day 5 %
		Day 6 %

My Nightly Recap 🌙

Amount of Time wasted _____

🙂 What went right?

I am grateful for...

☹ What went wrong?

Lead Generation notes:

_____

_____

_____

_____

_____

_____

_____

_____

_____

_____

_____

_____

What scripts/dialog worked? (build on this)

_____

_____

_____

_____

What lead generating activities did I enjoy / not enjoy? Why?

_____

_____

_____

_____

What inspired me today? (if nothing, what will I do different tomorrow?)

_____

_____

_____

_____

Day 62

Date _____ ⛺ _____ 🥤 _____

Hours available to work lead generation today _____

Activity	Actual	Goal	%	☺	😐	☹
Totals						

Running 6 day total
Day 1 _____ %
Day 2 _____ %
Day 3 _____ %
Day 4 _____ %
Day 5 _____ %
Day 6 _____ %

Supporting Tasks	Complete

My Nightly Recap 🌙

☺ What went right?

☹ What went wrong?

Amount of Time wasted _____

I am grateful for...

Lead Generation notes:

_____

_____

_____

_____

_____

_____

_____

_____

_____

_____

_____

_____

What scripts/dialog worked? (build on this)

_____

_____

_____

_____

_____

What lead generating activities did I enjoy / not enjoy? Why?

_____

_____

_____

_____

What inspired me today? (if nothing, what will I do different tomorrow?)

_____

_____

_____

_____

Day 63

Date _____ _____ _____

Hours available to work lead generation today _____

Activity	Actual	Goal	%	☺	😐	☹
Totals						

Running 6 day total
Day 1 _____ %
Day 2 _____ %
Day 3 _____ %
Day 4 _____ %
Day 5 _____ %
Day 6 _____ %

Supporting Tasks	Complete

My Nightly Recap

☺ What went right?

☹ What went wrong?

Amount of Time wasted _____

I am grateful for...

Lead Generation notes:

_____

_____

_____

_____

_____

_____

_____

_____

_____

_____

_____

_____

What scripts/dialog worked? (build on this)

_____

_____

_____

_____

What lead generating activities did I enjoy / not enjoy? Why?

_____

_____

_____

_____

What inspired me today? (if nothing, what will I do different tomorrow?)

_____

_____

_____

_____

Day 64

Date _____

Hours available to work lead generation today _____

Activity	Actual	Goal	%	☺	😐	☹
Totals						

Supporting Tasks	Complete

Running 6 day total
Day 1 _____ %
Day 2 _____ %
Day 3 _____ %
Day 4 _____ %
Day 5 _____ %
Day 6 _____ %

My Nightly Recap 🌙

☺ What went right?

☹ What went wrong?

Amount of Time wasted _____

I am grateful for...

Lead Generation notes:

_____

_____

_____

_____

_____

_____

_____

_____

_____

_____

_____

What scripts/dialog worked? (build on this)

_____

_____

_____

_____

What lead generating activities did I enjoy / not enjoy? Why?

_____

_____

_____

_____

What inspired me today? (if nothing, what will I do different tomorrow?)

_____

_____

_____

_____

Day 65

Date _____   _____   _____

Hours available to work lead generation today _____

Activity	Actual	Goal	%	☺	😐	☹		Running 6 day total	
								Day 1	%
								Day 2	%
								Day 3	%
								Day 4	%
Totals									
								Day 5	%

Supporting Tasks	Complete

Running 6 day total	
Day 6	%

My Nightly Recap

Amount of Time wasted _____

☺ What went right?

I am grateful for...

☹ What went wrong?

Lead Generation notes:

_____

_____

_____

_____

_____

_____

_____

_____

_____

_____

_____

_____

What scripts/dialog worked? (build on this)

_____

_____

_____

_____

What lead generating activities did I enjoy / not enjoy? Why?

_____

_____

_____

_____

What inspired me today? (if nothing, what will I do different tomorrow?)

_____

_____

_____

_____

Day 66

Date _____

Hours available to work lead generation today _____

Activity	Actual	Goal	%	☺	😐	☹
Totals						

Running 6 day total
Day 1 %
Day 2 %
Day 3 %
Day 4 %
Day 5 %
Day 6 %

Supporting Tasks	Complete

My Nightly Recap

☺ What went right?

Amount of Time wasted _____

I am grateful for...

☹ What went wrong?

Lead Generation notes:

_____

_____

_____

_____

_____

_____

_____

_____

_____

_____

_____

_____

What scripts/dialog worked? (build on this)

_____

_____

_____

_____

What lead generating activities did I enjoy / not enjoy? Why?

_____

_____

_____

_____

What inspired me today? (if nothing, what will I do different tomorrow?)

_____

_____

_____

_____

Congratulations! You did it!

By completing all 66 days you have set yourself on the right path that will take you to many years of success. You've also developed the "muscles" it takes to sustain your success for the long term. Nationally, over any given five-year period 85% of the agents fall out of the business, but you won't be one of them because you have done the work and created the discipline needed to be successful.

Now it's time to keep it going, Order another 66 day guidebook to stay on task for the next 66 days. You can order them from (fill in provider here) and contact me at Terry@WilsonRealtync.com for a copy of my tri-fold brochure you can carry with you, so you can keep up with your goals and your progress everywhere you go. Plus, I'd love to hear from you to see how you're doing and to get feedback from you because I know that I can always improve.

You may be wondering if this book is available as an app for your phone? I'm glad you asked. No there is no app because I don't want you getting lost in the trappings of your smart phone. Trust me on this. You and I both know that your phone calls to you. The apps call to you. A quick check of your calendar ends up two hours later watching cat videos. They are designed to grab your attention. Pen to paper will be done when you're done and there is no loss of data. Be quick with your notes and get back to lead generating. It is the most important thing you can do and the only thing you can do to truly build your business.

For a copy of our book Hiking the Real Estate Trail

For a copy of our book *Hiking the Real Estate Trail* please visit Amazon.com. This book will help you get your business up and running with clear guidance on what you need to do before you set off down the trail and the steps you need to take early in your hike. It will help you stay focused using goal setting and planning

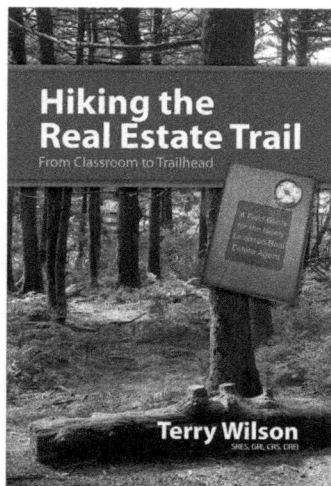

Hiking the Real Estate Trail
From Classroom to Trailhead

Terry Wilson
SRES, GRI, CRS, DRE

tips and help you understand how to develop your buyer and seller client base so you can close more transactions. It will assist you in learning the "call of the wild" and how to communicate with the various animals you meet along the way. And it provides guidance to help you complete this long journey where many before you have failed.

It's a guide that will assist you in deciding which firm to join, how to get started in the business, what to do in the first few weeks after you receive your license and advice to help you grow your business.

Just as with all hiking guides this book is meant to be marked up, scribbled on, copied and consulted regularly during your real estate hike. Throughout the book there are lined areas and several blank pages in the back for your notes, drawings, ah-ha moments and general musings.

It follows the structure of guide books; with the early chapters helping you to prepare for your hike and the later chapters showing you the various flora and fauna you will meet along your journey, the various trails you can take and what you should do each and every day to grow your business and become a better hiker.

Hiking
supplies

Tips & tricks

✓ If you want to buy back time, delete Facebook and Instagram and other social media platforms from your phone. Don't delete the settings, just the app icon. That way you can still check them by redownloading and it will remember who you are, but it will slow you down and force you to think about if you really need to be checking these social media platforms. You'll be amazed at the number of hours you'll buy back in a week.

✓ Seriously look at the number of hours you sleep. It may be difficult at first but getting up earlier can make a world of difference. Here's my routine. I go to bed usually around 10:30 then I'm up at 4:45 (my goal is 4:30, but, I'm a work in progress). I spend 10 minutes doing breathing meditation, I write in my journal and log what I'm grateful for. Then I read a business book for 30 minutes. At 6 AM I'm upstairs for a 30-minute workout. BOOM! By 6:30 I'm ready to go. Try it.

✓ The 20 second rule. If you want to develop a habit, make it 20 seconds easier. If you want to break a habit, make it 20 seconds harder. For example, if you want to start working out in the morning, get everything laid out the night before. If you're watching too much television (a huge time sucker) take the batteries out of the remote and put them in a drawer. You can still watch TV, but the act of having to get the batteries will give you a moment of pause and you'll find something more productive to do.

✓ Meditate. Meditate. Meditate. More and more research show just how powerful this simple habit can be. Simply sit with your eyes closed and focus on your breath. When your mind wanders (and it will) gently bring it back to your breath. Do this for 10 minutes.

✓ Write out your goals and review them first thing in the morning. Then meditate for a few minutes and see yourself achieving them. Make the image vivid. First class tickets to Paris because you just had your 10th closing? Not bad!!

✓ Layout what you're going to do tomorrow, tonight. Log your next day's activities the night before so you don't have to do it in the morning – there, you just bought back a good 15 minutes of morning productive time.

✓ Find an accountability buddy. Possibly another real estate agent or anybody in the field of sales. Contact each other regularly and help each other hike the trail every day. This is a very powerful way to assure you will get up every day and start hiking. No matter how tired you are, knowing that you have a fellow hiker with you will push you to keep going.

✓ Practice your ten second elevator speech. Imagine you are on an elevator and someone asks you what you do for a living. You now have ten seconds to explain what you do and why you do it to help them understand why they should work with you or why they should refer someone to you. These speeches can be very powerful and are certainly better than saying "I'm in real estate". In fact you should have a speech for your friends, family, and strangers. For a more detailed instruction on creating an elevator speech please see chapter 6 of Hiking the Real Estate Trail.

✓ Remember that your friends and family (your circle of influence) want to help you, but they won't remember what you do for a living so be sure to keep up with them regularly and remind them what you do and why you do it. In other words...

....

You must teach people how you want to be treated.

....

✓ If you work from home start each morning by making your bed and getting dressed for the "office".

✓ Try calendar blocking for a week. Block out junks of time to do certain tasks (especially if you work from home) and only do the task assigned to that block of time.

✓ Do not try to multi-task by starting a load of laundry while you get ready to make phone calls. Studies show that people don't multi-task as well as they think. Neither task gets done well and we waste a lot of time switching between the tasks.

✓ Give yourself a limited block of time to update social media. Set a timer on your phone so you don't get sucked into that world.

✓ Be wary about paying for companies to update social media on your behalf. I'm sure you've seen posts that you know the agent didn't post. People want to hear from you.

✓ Friends, family and past clients are your best source for leads. Don't worry about what to say or memorizing scripts and dialogs. Just be sure to contact them regularly. Make the conversation about them and listen for pain and pleasure points and how those might affect their, or someone they know, housing needs. Use the FORD technique (ask about Friends, Occupation, Recreation and Dreams).

✓ Here are some national statistics you'll want to be aware of:

- There are 15 transactions per year for every 100 households.

- On average each person in your database is worth $1,000/year. If you want to make $200,000/year then you must have 200 people you regularly contact.

- On average you lose 15% of your database each year, so you need to consistently add to your database of contacts.

50 Lead generating ideas that cost little to nothing

1. Regularly stay in touch with your existing clients.

2. Walk your neighborhood on Saturday mornings.

3. Wear your name tag everywhere (this is the most effective form of advertising!!!).

4. Call your friends and family no matter where they live.

5. Host a pampered Chef or Mary Kay party.

6. Join a networking group.

7. Join a school or government group.

8. Volunteer at a pet shelter.

9. Write note cards (minimal cost).

10. Host an open house (balloons and cookies).

11. Co-sponsor an open house with a lender (no cost).

12. Conduct a new-buyer seminar with other service providers.

13. Conduct a seller seminar.

14. Take donuts to a new construction model home. Get to know the on-site agent.

15. Regularly post on social media.

16. Start a blog.

17. Start a podcast (some cost here, but not until you grow).

18. Write articles for a local newspaper.

19. Give positive reviews for people you know on LinkedIn. (you help them, they'll want to help you).

20. Go to the same coffee house at the same time and day. You'll get to know the same crowd.

21. Have coffee with friends (go Dutch).

22. Instead of meeting friends for lunch, have a lunch gathering at your house.

23. Ask a friend to let you practice your listing and buyer presentations on them.

24. Be a guest on a AM Saturday morning talk show.

25. Teach a class for your local church or senior center.

26. If you have musical talent, think of ways to use that.

27. Volunteer for your neighborhood HOA.

28. Give a talk on career day at your local elementary school.

29. Coach little league or bring snacks.

30. Regularly attend little league games; either for your children or your neighbors' children.

31. Volunteer at your child's school.

32. Join a bike or hiking or another social club.

33. Join the Rotary or other networking group, more importantly become a leader in that group.

34. Volunteer to read at a local library or senior citizen center.

35. Ask to leave business cards at local businesses.

36. Treat your dentist, doctor and other vendors you regularly visit to some donuts.

37. Door knock your neighborhood and ask them what they would like to see in a newsletter you're planning to write. Plan to email so you'll need their email address.

38. Leave your business card at the restaurant and tip well.

39. Take homemade treats to local fire and police.

40. Be a greeter for your church so you get to meet people.

41. Boost your posts on Facebook (inexpensive).

42. Volunteer to help a blood drive.

43. Set up your profile on Zillow, Trulia and Realtor.com.

44. Answer questions on Zillow.

45. Set up a YouTube channel and make videos.

46. Regularly put fresh content on your website.

47. Ask to post other agent's listings on Facebook (be sure to credit them).

48. Write a home buying or selling book and self-publish.

49. Send birthday, anniversary, congratulations, home-buying anniversary and other special occasion hand-written cards.

50. Join groups on social media and occasionally mention something about real estate (maybe a new listing). You'll instantly increase the views.

51. Bonus tip: Purchase an inexpensive CRM that does automated email drip campaigns.

About the author

Terry Wilson was born and raised in Vestal, NY. He moved to Charlotte, NC in 1979. A graduate of UNC Charlotte, he joined IBM in 1981 where he discovered his true passion for teaching. In 1994 he joined a local personal computer training company and traveled the southeast teaching students the new world of Windows and the accompanying Microsoft products. Married and with a young son he wanted to spend more time at home and real estate seemed to be the answer. He successfully ventured into investment properties but soon turned to assisting others with buying and selling real estate. Over time, the teaching bug bit once again so he returned to the classroom.

Terry currently teaches pre-licensing and post-licensing courses and Continuing Education for Superior School of Real Estate and is the author of two Continuing Education courses; *Get into your Zone: a guide to zoning* and *Smooth Closings: from listing to contract, steps to take for a smooth closing.*

With his instructor hat on, Terry wrote and narrated *Hiking the Real Estate Trail: A guide to obtaining your license* – a popular audio CD book that provides licensure examination instruction and guidance to pre-licensing students.

Switching to his BIC hat, Terry wrote *Hiking the Real Estate Trail: From Classroom to Trailhead* – this thorough book guides newly licensed agents as they find their own way in the world of Real Estate.

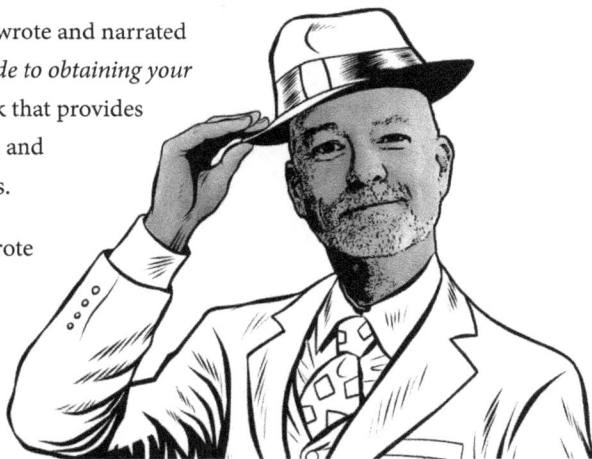

He holds the following designations: Certified Residential Specialist (CRS), Senior Real Estate Specialist (SRES), Graduate of Realtor Institute (GRI) and Distinguished Real Estate Instructor (DREI), a designation he is most proud of and one that is held by fewer than one hundred and twenty real estate instructors nationwide.

Terry is also Broker/Owner of Wilson Realty, a growing residential real estate firm with over 85 agents and four branch locations.

You can contact him at: Terry@WilsonRealtyNC.com

www.ingramcontent.com/pod-product-compliance
Lightning Source LLC
Chambersburg PA
CBHW021712210326
41599CB00013B/1622